Racism

A global political, economic and security parameter

ISBN-13: 978-1491028896
ISBN-10: 1491028890

Dedication

This book memorializes the billions of anonymous "losers" in the world who were born into poverty and died uneventful lives after enduring overwhelming hardships and suffering. Some may have felt it would have been better that they were never born. Many were victims of racism, racial nationalism and ethnic cleansing.

In addition, this book celebrates the relatively minuscule numbers of benevolent "winners" who were either born with platinum spoons in their mouths or had the luck and audacity to become wealthy beyond any commoner's wildest dreams and expectations. These have helped to make the world a better place.

Finally, it is the hope that the rest of the global wealthy elites will elect to contribute to efforts that will help to raise the tide of humanity that will guarantee abundance to all, and further increase their personal wealth many times over while reducing or eliminating the suffering of billions as a consequence of poverty.

Racism

A global political, economic and security parameter

Table of Contents

Chapter 1 – Race and racism

Section 1 - *What is race?*

The general consensus among current day anthropologists is "race" is a cultural construct and does not exist as a scientific fact or genetic variation. Their rationalization is that variation among individuals is far greater than between subgroups of *Homo sapiens* such as ethnic groups. This is primarily a politically correct motivated position by the professional anthropological and archaeological associations whose members are often funded by universities who receive federal funding who have conditions in place in regards to non-discrimination. It's an illusion to bury the evidence and facts. Perhaps anthropological groups worry that the paltry numbers of black anthropologists might subject their profession to accusations of racial bias, but if race doesn't exist, then racism can not be a factor why there are few black anthropologists and archaeologists.

Anyone with eyes open wide must recognize there are races among human beings, with lineages that can be traced both through archaeological evidence and DNA sequencing. Racial and ethnic differences are expressed not only in the difference in skin color, but other measurable differences that are generalized among various groups in higher proportions than in other groups that possess less of the genetic traits expressed as phenotypic attributes.

According to the American Red Cross, most Asians possess Rh-positive blood (98%+) while more than 18% of whites and 7% of blacks or Hispanics have Rh-negative blood, probably due to a higher historical degree of race mixing than among whites and Asians. Asians also have smaller stature and bone structure as compared to most African or European lineages, and the typical shape of the Asian skull is markedly different from white or black groups in the slope of the forehead, width and length of the nose, width versus length of the skull, shape of the jaw and prominence of the brow ridge in addition to the shape of the face (more circular), shape of the eyes, depth of the eye socket, distance between the eyes, and other distinguishing genetically evolved traits from environmental adaptations of their early ancestors.

So despite the politically correct position taken by anthropologists, as far as what almost all people in the world perceive, race exists. The fact that a light skin person can get a suntan or a dark skin person can lighten their skin using various chemical products doesn't change a person's race. Instead, what you end up with is a tanned white person like actor David Niven or a light skin singer like Michael Jackson. The fact that Michael Jackson had obvious plastic surgeries to whiten his nose and used chemicals to lighten his skin didn't change him from a "Negroid" to a "Caucasoid" and both black and white people will swear that Michael Jackson was born a black man and he died a black man.

Anthropologists are attempting to create an illusion that race does not exist, however any person on the street can distinguish between people of different races, except perhaps for mixed-race individuals whose genotype has become hybridized. Simple comparison is to recognize there are "pure breeds" of dogs and mixed breeds, or mutts. The same applies to humans. Where there are individuals whose genetic lineage reflects no breeding outside of their DNA pool, then their racial characteristics remain static. Consequently, Swedish people whose families have only interbred with Swedes will likely look light skinned, have blond hair, blue eyes and "Aryan" features, and look different from Asians or Africans. Let's stop pretending there's no such thing as race. The rare exception to racial phenotypes does not negate the larger generalized factual observations and DNA evidence that prove gene clusters exists for the different "pure" races that make them markedly different from each other.

Section 2 – *Natural genetic predisposed racism*

Now that we have established the fact that race exists as an obvious observable phenomenon that is based on the phenotypic expression of genetic differences that occur between subgroups of human beings, labeled as races, let's deal with the controversy in how different cultures view and treat racially different individuals and groups… the issue of racism.

Human beings are animals, and in many ways our natural drives, fears and behaviors reflect that exhibited by other mammals. Let's look at some of these universal behavior propensities common to almost all animals:

- Search for food and water – insufficient food and water results in weakening individuals, who then are more likely to fall prey to stronger competitors and predators.

- Fear of predators – without a reasonable level of fear, a false sense of security ensues that increases the probability of exposure to dangerous predators that can result serious injuries and therefore death.

- Fear of the unknown – without apprehension of the unknown and unfamiliar, there is no exercise of caution that results in a lack of concern and awareness of the environment that could have predators in hiding.

- Need for shelter – exposure to the elements subject individuals to great discomforts and extremes that wear the body down, stress out the immune system and make them visible to predators.

- Reproductive needs – insufficient birth rate over deaths results to eventual species extinction.

- Familial affinity – without the protection family, young individuals easily fall prey to larger stronger predators. Family members also give the love and nurturing that most mammals need when they are developing.

- Social interaction – Most mammals, including humans are primarily social animals and need the attention, validation and companionship of other people, though many find their relationship with their pet animals suffice.

- Activity – Boredom, monotony and tedium are the enemies of good mental and physical health because people are just designed that way through natural selection to be active in searching for food, shelter, avoiding predators, and either to retreat from adversaries or to attack their foes.

- Territoriality – Most mammals are territorial and will fight others of their own kind for possession, control and protection of their turf. This innate drive is an environmental survival adaptation to minimize competitors for the limited food supplies within their domain. Humans have taken this instinct even further through land ownership, marriage, and other cultural expectations.

- Dominance – In general, the higher testosterone level in men and their genetic construction predisposes them to struggle for dominance over females, children and other males. The competition for control and respect often leads to verbal and physical contests where the stronger, smarter, more clever, higher status, richer or more persistent person gets their way.

- Violence – Disputes that can't be resolved through discussion often end in violent confrontations. Violence is an emotional expression, usually of anger, but can be caused by fear or malevolence. Notice in the word, "malevolence", if broken down to its roots we get "male" and "violence." Men are ten times more likely to resort to violence than females, often without the initial or intermediary steps of verbal negotiation... straight to the sucker punch. The invention of guns has made it very convenient for even an otherwise fearful coward to become a "big man" in the eyes of his peers. Violence, like territoriality is a genetically evolved trait to enhance individual survival against competitors, predators and enemies.

- Rest and sleep – Everyone needs sufficient rest and rejuvenation to permit the body to recuperate and recover from exertion. Without time to rest and repair itself, the body eventually gets worn down and the immune system is more likely to fail against diseases that otherwise would not take hold.

- Discrimination – One basic survival instinct common to all animals is the ability to discern and identify potential predators, competitors and enemies who would do harm or threaten their territory or lives. Most wild animals have advanced olfactory senses and can literally sniff out their enemies. Humans instead rely primarily on visual cues, the most obvious being race. No wonder people of different races tend to feel wary, distrustful and suspicious of those from other races not of their own. It's a survival instinct.

In nature, all newborns automatically imprint on their parents and develop the needed discrimination ability to discern family from foe... friendly from predators. Humans have this same genetic propensity... infants imprint on their mothers or their caretakers, recognize and become comfortable with the racial appearance of whoever gives them food, comfort and security. No wonder if white children are raised around whites, blacks by blacks, and so on, those children feel most comfortable and safer around people of their own race. Why is it that even with existing government laws against "red lining" or not selling homes to non-whites in all white neighborhoods, that the vast majority of people prefer to live among others from their own race and ethnic groups? De facto segregation is real even if it's not government policy as in the past. Racial preference is real, even though miscegenation laws have been expunge from the books since WW2 in most places in America. Why is American still divided in racial lines? It's natural.

Section 3 – *Human culturally inculcated racism*

Human beings possess all of the behavioral tendencies common to almost all mammals and non-human primates. However, unlike other animals, humans possess a comparatively well-developed brain that allows them to create culture as an adaptive strategy to their environment. Culture comprises all of the social rules, political system, subsistence and economic system, migratory behavior, and technologies that allowed groups of individuals to beneficially adapt to their environments and to adjust to environmental changes, least become extinct like the Neanderthal and Cro-Magnon cousins of *Homo sapiens.*

It is in mankind's ability to create culture that enabled the development of racism, or treating individuals and subgroups differently based upon their perceived races. Other than skin color being the most obvious trait that can be seen from a distance, it caused racism to be primarily based on the most observable trait because it is easily recognizable and distinguishes individuals from one race to that of another. Racially hybridized individuals are a more recent phenomenon after removal of legal miscegenation barriers during the past century, along with the greater international mobility of people from different races, ethnic groups and cultures to interact and intermingle. As a greater number of mixed-race individuals will eventually be born, the issues of race and racism may lose its cultural significance, but that is likely another century away.

Racism is not only the identification of individuals from the different major races based on genetic make up that reflects the geographic origins of their original ancestors, it's the different values that society and people place on each race as compared to another. For example, in the book, 1984 by George Orwell, the society controlled by the state, Big Brother, had institutionalized the different races into a caste system, labeled as the Alphas, Betas, Gamma, Delta and Epsilon. Each level of the caste system reflected a variation of racial make-up and

8

socioeconomic status… not unlike the caste system traditionally in place in India as illustrated below:

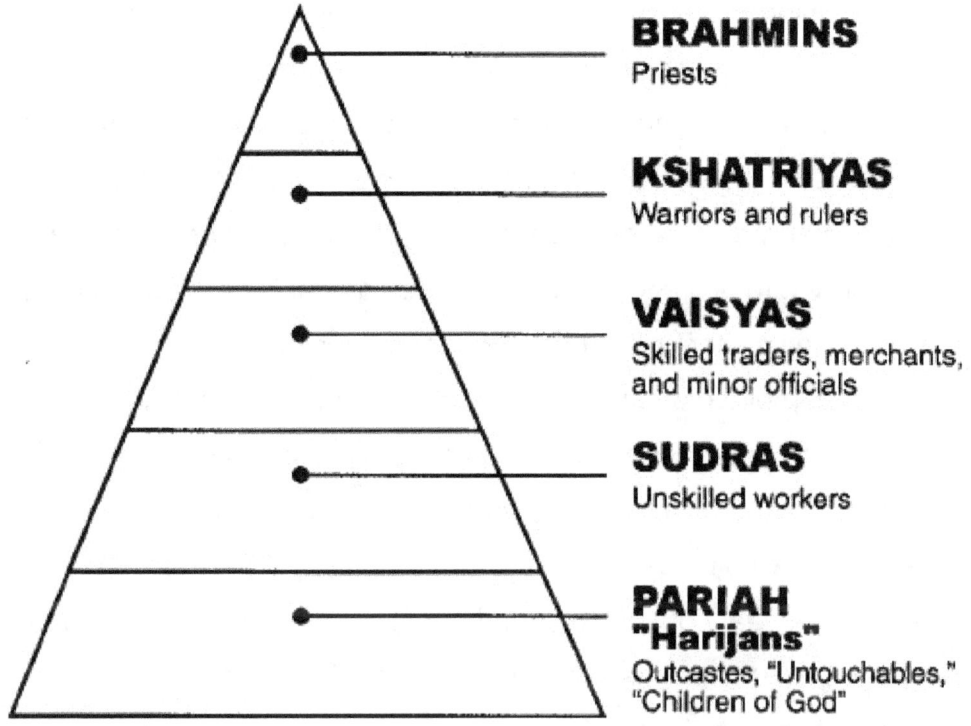

One of the basic principles of racism is the assignment of people to specific levels of the racial hierarchy in accordance to a social caste system. In the case of U.S. History, the racial caste system was based on skin color that resulted in assigned roles and occupations based on race. The white males were the privileged race and gender, the wealthy and powerful with the right to vote, own land and slaves. They were the Alphas. White women were the Betas whose role was to complement and be obedient to white men. The Gammas were the white merchants and service providers, the Deltas were the indentured immigrant servants and cheap laborers (e.g. Irish and Chinese), and the Epsilon were the black slaves who were sold like cattle.

How has modern society differed in the implementation of a racial caste system? Times have changed greatly in the past 50 years since the passage of the Civil Rights Act and subsequent non-discrimination legislation that affects almost every aspect of society. Yet, while no longer an institutionalized caste system due to the upward mobility provided by capitalism and entrepreneurism, a cursory observation of the race of individuals at each socioeconomic level of society clearly shows a similar pattern of race differentiation not unlike the traditional socioeconomic caste system.

The fact that the United States has an African-American President who was abandoned by his Kenyan father and raised by his Irish mother and Irish grandparents, who lived in Indonesia as a child and was for a time a practicing Muslim before he converted to Christianity (a religious crime punishable by death in some traditional Islamic states), has not changed one bit the stratification of American society primarily as a de facto consequence of race. President Obama is the token symbolic expression of the non-racism ideal that is promoted by news media and the education system based on laws on the books.

The largest group of the most powerful and richest people in America continues to be white men, and whose white wives receive substantial wealth while married and in divorce. Even though women complain that their average income still falls around 20% below that of the average income for men, if we look objectively at education, years of seniority, and equal performance levels, women are indeed on par with men... as men don't take years off their careers to have babies and to care for them in their early years before returning to the work force. White men continue to be the Alphas, and their women, the Betas.

The next level of society are the Gammas... mostly white professionals whether male or female, but increasingly, educated and entrepreneurial individuals from other races who have been able to acquire a modicum level of wealth and political clout through their talents and professions. The Deltas are the recent immigrants, mostly undocumented who provide unskilled labor to fill the manual jobs the Gammas would prefer not to touch. Finally, there are the Epsilons, who are primarily the descendants of African slaves and a more recent phenomenon, Hispanic gangs who are descendants of immigrants. The Epsilon class of society is comprised of the predominantly poor, undereducated, low skilled sector of the impoverished populace who rely on government programs, charity, and crime as their source of subsistence.

Socioeconomic class continues to play a huge role in the upward mobility of individuals and specifically who assigned members choose to associate with in their social networks. Alphas primarily rub elbows with other Alphas, while their Beta spouses become the socialites of high society. The Gammas join professional associations to network their careers and to gain mutual validation of

10

their value to society. The Deltas try to remain anonymous, because being unknown is being un-owned and not deportable. Finally, the Epsilon fill our nation's jails and prisons, that gives Gamma professionals full time employment.

Even though over the past two decades, media has attempted to depict racial minorities in more diverse roles, and less in traditionally stereotypical roles, the reality still exist that stereotypes die hard because sufficient statistics seem to support some aspects of racial stereotypes. For example, blacks tend to be violent, and sure enough they are disproportionately represented in our nation's prisons for the commission of violent crimes. Asians are good at math. Even though I personally am a poor to mediocre mathematician, and my African-American brother-in-law graduated from UCLA with a Masters Degree in mathematics, we are the exceptions to the stereotypes... the social rules. Perhaps it's because George Zimmerman (a Hispanic Jew who is classified as a white man) shot and killed Travon Martin (an African-American teen) because he was afraid this black guy was going to kill him. Stereotypes die slowly and die hard... and too many people needlessly die because of it.

Section 4 – *Politically based racism*

Speaking of the Zimmerman trial and his acquittal, were Zimmerman an African-American as was Travon Martin, the new media would likely have never picked up this story and woven it into a race issue. Consequently, had President Obama not injected the issue of race into the public arena by stating that if he had a son, he would likely look like Travon, then the issue of racial profiling and racism would probably not have taken hold in the black community. On average Blacks kill 15,000 blacks every year in America, along with 1,600 white and Hispanic people and hundreds of Asians and mixed race people. When blacks kill people from other races, the media and government never interjects the race card. But when a black person is killed by a non-black person or by the police, race and racial profiling is almost always blamed as the mitigating circumstance leading to death. I find that to be incredulous, out of context, and statistically fraudulent... a lie that perpetuates racial disharmony, racial stereotypes, and interracial hatred among the populace.

If Anthropologists are correct, and race doesn't exist biologically or by the known classification methodology that groups all humans into the *Homo sapiens* species, then why does government institutionalize specific racial categories and force them on people at all levels of public programs, including education, census, employment, and other government programs? Consequently, people are encouraged to vote by racial groups to create voting blocks for similar race candidates who share their subcultures and values. A cursory examination of voting records in relation to race clearly show non-whites prefer voting for non-whites and people of varying races tend to vote for their own race… specifically, blacks vote for blacks, Hispanics for Hispanics, Asians for Asians and whites for whites.

When race is not an issue due to the forced choice two-party option system, voters will cast their votes to reflect their parties, liberal versus conservative views and the various issues in the political spectrum. In the absence of a viable white candidate in any particular party, and a minority candidate appears viable due to charisma, persuasiveness and popularity, liberal whites have shown they will vote for non-white candidates. Conservatives and Republicans continue to pursue their traditional whiteness paradigm more often than not, and in major elections where there are sufficient non-white populations, they have lost whenever younger and liberal whites joined non-whites to vote for viable non-white candidates, such as Barrack Obama. Even with their failure to depose Obama in 2012, the GOP still continues their primarily white preference and exclusivity program.

The bi-partisan comprehensive immigration legislation passed by the Senate does not appeal to Republican members in the House because the grass root white voter who live in the "red states" don't support any non-white agendas proposed by liberal lawmakers and Obama. The major sticking point is a path to citizenship for all illegal immigrants currently in the United States. Republicans object to the inclusion of upwards of 14 million illegal immigrants eventually becoming citizens because statistics clearly show minority group voters will usually vote for liberal politicians who favor government entitlement programs that conservatives feel are socialistic entitlement programs mostly paid for by white citizens (whites foot the bill for 85% of welfare programs). Legalizing 12 to14 million illegal Hispanics will only add huge numbers of voters for the Democratic

Party. Perhaps, there should be no path to citizenship, but instead permanent residency can be earned by passing specific rational non-race based benchmarks. The Tea Party would be more receptive to that proposal as long as permanent residency does not lead to citizenship, but they would likely also stipulate that the natural born children of such "amnesty" candidates could never become citizens. Are ultra-conservative Republicans actually motivated by racial discrimination? Would they vehemently raise so many objections to comprehensive immigration reform if the vast majority of "amnesty" applicants were English or Germanic? There's probably a hidden element of racism that motivates their objections that go beyond their concern that new illegal immigrant turned voters would likely support Democratic candidates. It seems they don't trust the government to protect their political and economic interests.

Americans continue to distrust their government, with only 34% expressing trust in government (McIntosh & Parker, pg.1). Disillusionment with political leaders and dissatisfaction with the way government performs its duties are essential factors that cause distrust of government. However, distrust of government and discontent is not fostering a disregard for the nation's laws, eroding patriotism or discouraging government service, suggesting Americans are frustrated with government rather than angry with it (M&P, pg.2). Consequently, even though 38% of a small segment who are most angry at government could see justification for violent acts against the federal government (M&P, pg.3), there is no indication that these attitudes are near a crisis stage (M&P, pg.1) to become a threat to our democratic government.

Even during the height of President Clinton's scandalous charges of adultery and perjury, trust declined only modestly (5%) in public opinion polls suggesting that distrust of government is more often connected to how people feel about the overall state of the nation (M&P, pg.1). However, studies also appear to indicate that distrust of political leaders and lack of faith in the political system are principal reasons the public distrust government. It also appears that cynicism about political leaders and the political system is more crucial to distrust than concerns about the proper role of government, worries about its power and intrusiveness, misgivings about its priorities, or resentment about taxes (M&P,

pg.5)

Furthermore, the PEW Research Center found in November 1996 that over 60% of survey respondents believed an increase in pessimism about the country's future was due to increasing problems with crime, drugs, and low moral and ethical standards. Perceived level of crime appears to have an opposite correlation on trust, i.e. more murders, less trust (M&P, pg.6). There also appears the potential effect of electoral cynicism and alienation. Academic researchers seek to discover potential causalities in the political culture of our nation to determine the meaning and likely future manifestations of decreasing public trust of our representational democratic system. Does the decline in trust indicate a loss of support for incumbency or for the democratic system? (L&G pg.140). The current level of political trust has steadily declined since 1964 (L&G pg. 137) indicating a steady decline of public trust in government from the 75% level during 1958-64 to recent 20-30% levels, except for the Reagan era when trust rose to the 40% level (F&Z pgs.13,15). The issue of "trust to do right" is described by Klosko (pg. 108) as a concept of perception of legitimacy and personal benefits. Individuals insist on personal interpretations of the same concept (Mason, pg.78), which is evidenced by the tendency of voters to trust the politicians that they elected versus those of the opposing party. In addition Mason (pg. 11) describes the effects of public culture on the perception and expectation of justice as a requisite of trust (Mason, pg. 111).

The relationship between political trust and system stability is thought to be causal by political scientists such as Arthur Miller (L&G pg.140). The decline of trust in government is thought have a potentially negative effect on system stability, however, no empirical evidence lends credence to the view that democratic governance is threatened by floundering trust in the federal government. Are, as Dr. Miller opined, higher levels of distrust for the political system a precursor of "great danger for the American system of government." or is lower trust levels even threatening? (L&G pg. 140).

Analysis of a question posed by NES interviewers, "How much of the time do you trust the federal government to do right?" attempts to measure the public's attitude toward the democratic system. NES data is cross tabulated against other

14

variables that may have a causal correlation with this issue (i.e., SES variables). The federal government referred to in the question is generally agreed to mean the executive and legislative branches.

This paper cross tabulates the question, "How much of the time do you trust the federal government to do right?" using the 1996 NES data base to measure the public's level of trust in government, and whether SES variables differentially modify the reported levels of trust. The hypotheses being tested are that 1) Asian-Americans are more likely to have a higher trust in government than either African-American or white voters; 2) greater trust in government is more likely to occur when respondents feel good about their financial situation; 3) older voters tend to have greater trust in government than younger voters; and, 4) higher levels of information about politics and public affairs leads to increased trust in government. The data results are controlled for gender differences.

Political theorists have advanced causal relationships between levels of trust and variables that include levels of knowledge (Mason, pg.107), gender differences (Mason, pg.127), and SES (Parker, pg.446).

The cross tabulation of 1996 NES appear to suggest certain SES demographic factors are likely to have a direct correlation to a higher or lower than expected level of *trust in government*. Among these hypothesized direct correlates are the following variables:

1. **Table 1: Race**. Data indicates that Asian-Americans are more likely to have a higher trust in the federal government than African-Americans and whites. A Chi sq. of (p=0.00) is statistically significant in supporting the data that 44% of Asian-Americans compared to 28% of whites and blacks trust the federal government to do right "just about always" or "most of the time". A tau-b of -.02 indicates insignificant interaction between dependent variable of trust" and independent variable of "race".

2. **Table 2: Financial Situation**. A statistically significant probability does not appear to exist according to how respondents viewed their financial situation as a correlate of their level of trust in the government, with approximately 26% to 29% (28.6% average) feeling trust in government "just about always" or "most of the time." A Chi sq. value of (p=0.01) and a Tau-b value of 0.0 confirm a non-

interactive correlation between respondents' financial situation and "trust".

3.   **Table 3: Age**. Elderly voters in retirement age (65 and older) tend to have greater trust in government than younger voters, with 37.6% expressing "trust" just about always or most of the time, as compared to 29.4% for ages 18-29, 24.9% for the 30-49 group, and 28.4% for ages 50-64. The results are statistically significant, with a Chi sq. of (p=0.00) that validates the 8% to 13% difference between voters in retirement age (over 65) and the rest of the population. A Tau-b of -.05 shows a very low correlation between the age and trust variables.

4.   **Table 4: Information Level**: No statistically significant difference in respondent measures on the question of trust was found due to the level of information about politics and public affairs; however, the data suggests a small but gradual trend in lessening "trust" in correlation to higher information levels (Chi sq. of p=0.12), and Tau-b = -.05.

5.   **Table 5: Gender**: No significant differences in respondent measures on the   question of trust was found due to gender differences. A Chi sq. of (p=0.83) and Tau-b of -.01 indicate no statistically significant relationship between this control variable and the dependent variable of "trust in the federal government".

6.   **Table 5a: Race as Independent Variable, Controlled for Gender**:   There appears to be a statistically significant difference in the apparent "race" effect for Asian-American males on the question of trust, reporting a Chi sq. of (p=0.00) and a variance of 6.5% to 9.5% more trust in government "just about always" or "most of the time" when compared to whites or blacks. A Tau-b of 0.0 indicates virtually no interaction between the variables. In the case of Asian-American females, 52% trusted government in the two top categories stated, as compared to 28.5% to 30.4% for whites and blacks respectively. The results are statistically significant with a Chi sq. of (p=0.0) and Tau-b of -.04, indicating low interaction between the dependent and independent variables.

7.   **Table 5b: Age as Independent Variable, Controlled for Gender**:   There does not appear to be a statistically significant

16

(Chi sq. of p=0.21) difference in the apparent "age" effect for males on the question of trust, even though a variance of 4.7% to 11.8% existed between those 65 or older and younger respondents, with a Tau-b of –0.4, indicating insignificant interaction between the variables. In the case of females, there appears to be a statistically significant "age" differential in the response to trust between those 65 and over as compared to those younger than 65, with a Chi sq. of (p=0.02) and a variance of 11%-13% for seniors who trusted government "just about always" or "most of the time." The Tau-b for the males was -.04 and –0.6 for females, indicating a slight multivariate interaction.

In addressing the NES question asked respondents, "Do you trust the federal government to do right?", various independent studies suggest correlation between trust and political obligation (Klosko, pg. 8-10), the effects of public culture (Mason, pg. 10), justice (Mason, pg. 11), and fairness (Klosko, pg.128-129). Other political theorists have advanced causal relationships between levels of trust and variables that include understanding of democracy (Mason, pg. 85), expectations (Kimball, pg.715), perception of crime, scandals, and the state of the economy (Chanley, pg.247), alienation and presidential performance (Erber & Lau), and incumbency (Parker, pg.445).

This paper's assessment of NES data does not support a causal relationship between trust and level of knowledge of political information or gender differences. Furthermore, Parker (pg.446) concludes that it is difficult to establish any hypothesized relationship between SES and trust based on previous research due to the ambiguous nature of the findings. For example, some findings indicate that while distrust of government was higher among the lower SES classes, other studies concluded that higher-status groups were more alienated than lower-status groups. Still other studies found no relationship between social class and trust.

Kimball (pg.721) confirmed that participation, income, and political knowledge do not significantly affect the candidacy factor scores, while both partisanship and support for a popular president bears positive effects on congressional approval and trust for government. The cross tabulation of NES data confirms that no statistically significant correlation could be found to link income or political knowledge directly to levels of trust in government.

In the absence of consensus, it is hypothesized that a positive relationship exists between trust in their own elected representatives and socioeconomic status; in other words, each SES group would trust their representatives while distrusted the elected officials of other groups that they do not identify with (Parker, pg.446-7). Parker also expected higher levels of system trust to contribute to higher levels of trust in incumbent representatives, adding that one's own economic plight and government waste are two common economic complaints may contribute to levels of trust in one's elected representative (pg.445).

Only two measures, "race" (Asian-American females) and "age" (R's 65 or over) appear to suggest statistically significant values to the variances from other categories in their data set. In light of the fact that upwards of one-third of Asians and Asian-American females marry outside their race in the U.S., we may surmise that their value for the American people, culture and democracy tends to be generally high, resulting in a higher level of trust for the federal government. In the case of retirees 65 and over, we suggest that their eligibility for government monetary benefits (Social Security and Medicare) may tend to encourage more favorable attitudes in the federal government, and their regular receipt of monthly checks would certainly tend to favor more trust than distrust. Other potential explanations for the significantly higher level of government trust attributable to both Asian-American females and the elderly may reflect their greater tendency to have "at-home" lifestyles, where issues of crime and violence tend to be less than for the general population who are more interactive in the public and exposed to greater social perils.

Chanley (pg.247) hypothesized that as the proportion of the public who perceive crime as the nation's most important problem rises, trust in government will fall. While Chanley (pg.239-240) stated that while responsibility for changes in government trust levels has been attributed to a variety of causal factors (economic, social-cultural, or political), scholars suggest that trust in government is influenced by the performance of the national economy and citizens' evaluations of the economy, as negative perceptions of the economy promote greater distrust. Second, declining trust has been attributed to social-cultural factors such as rising crime and child poverty. Finally, changes in trust in government have been linked to numerous political factors, including citizens' evaluation of incumbents and institutions, an increasing number of political scandals and increased media focus on political corruption and scandal.

Chanley (pg.239-40) suggest that negative perceptions of the economy (not personal finances), scandals associated with Congress (not information level), and increasing public concern about crime each lead to declining public trust in government consistent with the contention that trust in the federal government is more closely tied to trust in Congress than to the president, they found that allegations of misconduct on the part of Congress exert greater influence on trust in government than do allegations of misconduct by the executive. She concludes that the literature suggests that declining trust in government is a complex phenomenon with multiple potential causes (pg.240).

Parker (pg.442) describes the decline in the influence of political parties as having elevated the importance of voter trust in incumbent public officials. This increased attention is evidenced by elected officials having to spend considerable time encouraging their constituents to "trust them", and that trust in incumbents ultimately influences electoral support for the government. Consequently, Parker (pg.443) believes that a trustworthy legislator, therefore, gains the loyalty of his constituents, stating, "Thus, we believe that trust in a legislator is predicated on the belief that the representative is serving, and will continue to serve, the best interests of his or her supporters rather than acting out of self interest is consistent with a description of constituent trust."

Chanley hypothesized that trust in government is thought to reflect public satisfaction with political leaders and institutions. When presidential and congressional evaluations are favorable, trust in government is expected to increase. Similarly negative evaluations are expected to result in lower levels of trust; however these expectations were not confirmed by their results. Neither presidential nor congressional approval exerts any causal influence on trust… suggesting that presidential and congressional evaluations are as much a consequence of trust in government as they are a cause (pg.251).

Trust may simply boil down to the tendency of people on the losing side in an election to have lower levels of satisfaction with the system than do those on the winning side. Political scientists are interested in attempting to evaluate the patterns of trust, alienation, and antigovernment sentiment with our democracy is to ascertain the potential threshold at which respect for the system may plummet below "a point of no return." In analyzing the electoral landscape, demographic, attitudinal and political culture are examined and cross-sectioned to determine if there are clear indicants of verifiable predictors of citizens' political behaviors. A cross tabulation of NES (National Election Survey) data from the NES sampling Previous political science research literature and studies have not explained these variances adequately, and any inter-dependencies may be difficult to conclude.

Kimball (pg.722), instead, suggests that citizens appear to make comparisons between what they expect their elected representatives in congress to be like and what they perceive these representatives actually are like, indicating citizens disapprove of congress when they're not getting the congress they want (with honest, community-minded members); or because they feel they're getting a congress they don't want (inhabited by partisan, career-oriented, lawyer legislators).

In our two-party competitive system, the political culture encourages and needs both loyalty and dissent. It is the absence of disruptive acts by a substantial portion of society and not the presence of supportive attitudes that is essential for maintaining an established democracy (F&Z pg. 23-24). Consequently, it is doubtful that distrust of government alone could be a threat to the American system, an opinion supported by Citrin who felt that distrustful individuals were not ready to repudiate the American form of government (L&G pg. 141). Moreover L&G (pg.24) observed that the public perception that "government leaders were corrupt and served primarily special interest groups" contributes to lower trust in government. F&Z (pg.12-13) observed "...in general, the public has considerable confidence in the institutions of government but not much confidence in the individuals charged with operating these institutions."

Anderson (pg.67) observed that "low levels of citizen support can pose serious problems for democratic systems because both their functioning and maintenance are intimately linked with what and how people think about democratic governance", adding, "... alienation from the issues by both major parties of candidates will lead to declining trust in government we also find evidence that political cynicism is associated with greater approval of anti-government protest...." Prolonged discontent and alienation from the political system many challenge its legitimacy and, ultimately, its very existence. Political participation through the established channels may decrease, and constituents may be tempted to support radical political solutions.

According to Miller, those who disproved of both the Democratic and the Republican policy alternatives in 1968 were the most cynical...Citrin argued that it was dissatisfaction with incumbent leaders rather than their policies that made people cynical. Political scientist study trust in government because (in theory) it reflects on the stability of a country's government. People who distrust their system of government, who do not view it as legitimate are supposedly more prone to antigovernment activities. Research data tend to support this notion of legitimacy, but only as it applies to citizens who display chronic personal feelings about politics.

The data clearly shows that people with personal political chronicity are more likely to legitimize anti-government feelings and actions. Moreover as predicted, a clear pattern appears in the data: the more difficult each activity is to approve, the stronger the relationship with political cynicism.

Approval of legal protests: $P = <.10$ (no issues or personal chronicity)

$P = .12$ (with personal chronicity)

Approval of disobeying unjust laws $= .15$ ($p<.05$) with personal chronicity.

Approval of trying to stop government operations $= .21$ ($p<.01$) with personal chronicity.

The author describes people with chronically accessible issues schema as those who think about politics primarily in terms of the issues at stake and the policies drafted to deal with them. They evaluate presidential candidates in terms of the issue stands they take. People with personal schema chronicity think about politics and evaluate candidates primarily in terms of the personality characteristics of candidates.

The basic argument is dissatisfaction with the policy alternatives offered by the two major parties or their leaders causes cynicism, which naturally leads to governmental distrust as evidenced by a greater likelihood to legitimize antigovernment feelings and activities. Those who perceive themselves as distant to the issue stands of both the incumbent and the challenging candidate or party will be the most cynical, especially for people with an issues chronicity. They will interpret the trust in government items more in terms of the policies being carried out by those in government and those who disapprove of the ways in which the incumbent handles the job will be most dissatisfied.

A cross tabulation of NES (National Elections Study) data from the year 1996 discloses various correlations between dependent and independent variables, suggesting speculative support of hypotheses that have foundation in previous political science research literature and studies. Explaining the variances and inter-dependencies may be more difficult and conclusions would likely fall short of the criteria for recognition of irrefutable "principles"; however, hypotheses will be ventured as potentially plausible causation of political opinion.

In addressing the NES question asked respondents, "Do you trust the federal government to do right?", the question itself must first be defined in terms of public understanding in respect to popular and political culture. Furthermore, certain factors that contribute to the development of trust or lack thereof should be considered, including political obligation (Klosko, pg. 8-10), the effects of public culture (Mason, pg. 10), justice (Mason, pg. 11), and fairness (Klosko, pg.128-

129). Other political theorists have advanced causation relationship between levels of trust and variables that include levels of knowledge (Mason, pg. 107), gender differences (Mason, pg. 127), understanding of democracy (Mason, pg. 85), expectations (Kimball), perception of crime, scandals, and the economy (Chanley), alienation and presidential performance (Erber & Lau), and incumbency (Parker).

My review of the NES data, political and social science theories and culture, the dynamic state of public opinions, and the imperfections of opinion-based research techniques lead me to interpret with caution any statistically significant conclusions that might otherwise be suggested by an analysis of the NES study, or any study based solely on internalized emotionally-based mentations that typify respondents' understanding of, and answers to diversity of interviewers, who by the fact of their gender, appearance, tone, and mannerisms may have affected the honesty level and very nature of the answers received.

The hypotheses tested by cross tabulations of 1996 NES data are:

1. **Race**. It is likely that Asian-Americans have a higher trust in government, and African-Americans feel a lower trust in government than the white electoral majority.

2. **Income Level**. Greater trust in government is likely to occur at the higher income levels.

3. **Age**. Older voters tend to have greater trust in government than younger voters.

4. **Educational Level**. A higher educational levels general correlates to a higher level of information about politics and public affairs, which is likely to increase trust in government.

5. **A higher level of satisfaction** with the way that democracy works in the U.S. and the federal government's handling of most important problems is likely to result in a higher trust level in government.

Dependent variable: "How much of the time do you trust the federal government to do right?" [v960566].

Independent variables: Race [v960067]; Education level [v960070]; Income level [v960076]; Age [v960605]; and, [v961142]; Satisfaction with government

Control Variables for all hypotheses will be:

1. Gender [v960066].
2. Alienation; "People like me don't have much say in government". [v961245].

Public perceptions and understanding of apparently simple ideas such as trust, rightness, and governance varies and may be a muddle of presuppositions based upon perceived popular and political culture. Is the concept of "rightness" defined in terms of what voters perceive as a moral value when applied to their judgment of the federal government's actions? The definition of rightness in social and political contexts is situational and relative to each individual's degree of assimilation of the dominant social and cultural values of the majoritarian institutions, including schools, media, religious faiths, and public law. In its daily practice, the perception of rightness is rather a personal edifice based in part upon parental transmission, religious beliefs, and popular culture, with ample rationalization or denial when one's own actions may contradict one's moral opinions and self-image. Consequently, in attempting to explain the NES data set and any variances or lack thereof, the reader should keep in mind the subjectivity of respondents' answers to the question posed by NES interviewers, i.e., "How much of the time do you trust the federal government to do right?" Klosko (pg. 108) discussed the concept of relative rightness and how its perception varied according to perceptions of legitimacy and personal benefits.

Trust is another one of those non-definitive terms that appear to span a gradient in terms of social-political contexts. If an individual were asked if they trust their parents, more likely than not, most people would answer affirmatively. However, that's not to say that any individual would necessary trust their parents with their money, or car, or children, or financial decisions. Yet they could answer emphatically that they in fact trust their parents. The subjectively quantifiable aspects of trust also create a dilemma for data interpretation. How much does a person trust, is like the proverbial, how much does a person love another? Is love and trust absolute concepts, either in theory or practice? I venture to say not.

Finally, "who" or "what" is the federal government? Ask a hundred people and it could mean a dozen different things. After all, the NES interviewers weren't questioning only academicians, who as a group would probably agree somewhat more than the usually disinterested, alienated, apathetic, un-informed or misinformed public, who were the respondents in the study. Is the federal government the executive branch, and if so, do respondents point to the presidency or to the actions of his cabinet, or vice president? Is the federal government also inclusive of the legislative and judicial branches? Is the federal government its bureaucratic agencies, such as the IRS, DEA, CIA, and FBI? Or is the public's concept and definition of the federal government that isolated body of public officials so caught up in mutual and self-aggrandizement that they don't even know there's a world outside of Washington D.C.? Individuals insist on personal and often different interpretations of the same concept (Mason, p.78).

In order to make some sense of the NES data set, the reader should set aside personal definitions of "trust", and "rightness" and "the federal government". The reader should attempt to imagine what the majoritarian's perceived definition of each concept meant when they responded to NES interviewers. Consequently, since there is no effective method to measure or to understand what respondents really meant when they answered the question, "How much of the time do you trust the federal government to do right?", then let's rely on popular notions of "trust", "rightness", and the "federal government", whatever that might mean to non-political scientists. According to J. Rawls, a political theorist (Mason, pg.10). In addition Mason (pg. 11) describes the effects of public culture on the perception and expectation of justice as a requisite of trust, and further observes the ethics of rights and rightness (Mason, pg. 111) as an interactive contingency between the moral precepts of political culture and the individual's personal self-assessment against those perceived standards.

It is obvious that political research and political science are not scientific endeavors in the sense of physics, chemistry, biology or rocket science. While the NES study attempts to apply the "scientific method" and research methodologies that typify and define the sciences (i.e., observation, data collection, analyses, hypothetical and theoretical construct, repetitive verifiability, conclusions and discovery of principles), the primary instrument of political science research, "public opinion surveys", is too unexacting to provide much more than conjecture and rudimentary conclusions that are generally insufficiently based on factual constructs to provide definitive bases for theory building or reliable predictions.

Having disclosed these short-comings, it appears the results of the cross tabulation of NES data (1996) neither supports, refutes, or is conclusive in regards to the assessment of previous studies and theories to explain the results of the dependent and independent variables contained in the study.

References

Andersen, Christopher J., and Christine A. Guillory. *Political Institutions and Satisfaction with Democracy: A Cross-National Analysis of Governmental Majoritarian Systems.* The American Political Science Review, Vol. 91, No. 1 (Mar. 1997), pp. 66-81.

Barnes, Samuel H., and Max Kaase. *Political Action.* Beverly Hills, CA: Sage Publications, Inc., 1979.

Brodney, Jeffrey L. *Building Trust in Government.* Journal of Public Administration Research and Theory, Vol. 6, Issue 3 (July 1996), pp. 486-491.

Chanley, Virginia A., Rudolph, Thomas A., and Wendy M. Rahn. *The Origins and Consequences of Public Trust in Government: A Time Series Analysis.* Public Opinion Quarterly, Vol 64, (2000), pp. 239-256.

Epstein, Jeffrey H. *American Distrust Their Government.* Futurist, Vol 32, Issue 7 (Oct. 1998), pp. 12-13.

Erber, Ralph, and Richard R. Lau. *Political Cynicism Revisted: An Information-Processing Reconciliation of Policy-Based and Incumbency-Based Interpretations of Changes in Trust in Government.* American Journal of Political Science, Vol 34, No. 1 (Feb. 1990), pp. 236-253.

Harris, Paul. *Civil Disobedience.* Lanham, MD: University Press of America, Inc., 1989.

Kimball, David C., and Samuel C. Patterson. *Living Up to Expectations: Public Attitudes Toward Congress.* The Journal of Politics, Vol 59, No. 3 (Aug. 1997), pp. 701-728.

Klosko, George. *The Principle of Fairness and Political Obligation.* Lanham, MD: Rowman & Littlefield Publishers, Inc., 1992.

Mason, Andrew. *Explaining Political Disagreement.* NY, NY: Cambridge University Press, 1993.

McIntosh, Mary, and Kimberly Parker. *Deconstructing Distrust How Americans View Government.* Princeton, NJ: The Pew Research Center For The People & The Press, 2001.

Parker, Suzanne L., and Glenn R. Parker. *Why Do We Trust Our Congressman?* The Journal of Politics, Vol. 55, No. 2 (May 1993), pp 442-453.

Section 5 – The racism of poverty

Who are most likely to express racial prejudice and believe in racial stereotypes? Who are most likely to dislike, discriminate, ridicule, exclude and hate people from other races? The general formula is rather universal and basic, including the following factors:

- Being poor subjects people to desperate conditions, forcing them to eek out subsistence by supplementation through criminal activities. The primary reason for a higher crime rate among impoverished unemployed people who disproportionately represent racial minorities due to the socioeconomic structure of widespread subtle covert racism is their very limited options to advance themselves due to their dire circumstances.

- Living among impoverished people is tough because unlike middle class people who possess their fill of material comforts, poor people who want things and can't afford them resort to buying stolen property, burglarize, steal or rob their neighbors in their own and adjoining communities.

- Living in blighted communities results from the lack of property ownership and consequently destroying things that have no personal stake is easy to do, especially when expressing dissatisfaction, frustration and desire to lash out at symbols of a prosperous society that left them behind.

- Enduring repeated violence, particularly when growing up is commonplace for children who are subjected to frequent bullying, beatings and sometimes stray bullets. In response to the high level of physical violence, verbal abuse, and living under the constant threat of violence, many individuals turn to gangs for mutual respect and protection and instead of becoming a calming example, they are instead caught up in reinforcing the cycle of violence where past victims become future perpetrators and predators.

- Poor education, especially in our increasingly highly technical society is a severe obstacle to finding substantive career opportunities. Employers are only interested in hiring people they feel can learn and understand the needs and requirements of their businesses. An uneducated individual does not possess the knowledge and skills that the vast majority of hiring managers seek, and therefore their remaining options usually take on the path to criminal activities.

- Parental and other kinship modeling and pressure is a sure way to place otherwise innocent malleable children either on to positive or negative life paths. If by the time a child is school aged and has already witnessed their parents verbally and physically abusing each other, committing repeated incidents of child abuse against them and their siblings, abusing illegal drugs and indulging excessively in alcohol induced speech and behaviors, the rest of a child's life will likely be an uphill emotional and mental battle, to compound the physical and dietary challenges of poverty.

- Peer group validation modeling and pressure is probably the single most important factor to influence and shape teenage values and behaviors. Following "the wrong crowd" most often leads to juvenile detention camps, or worse results in getting tried for adult crimes as a minor and sent to adult prisons for their adult lives.

- Alcohol and drug abuse are the two most pernicious factors in destroying lives because it removes the ability to make rational decisions. While under the influence of drugs or alcohol, relationship problems develop and persist, leading to job-related conflicts and poor performance. Not only poor people abuse drugs and alcohol, but it's a relative cheap escape from a miserable life while they are under the influence because they can't afford Disneyland.

- Well educated people, well traveled people and people with sufficient income and comfortable lifestyles are less likely to be racist. Why? The exposure to the knowledge of a more diverse range of humanity tends to broaden a person's understanding, acceptance and reference points about race that enables them to reject erroneous racial stereotypes, but instead to recognize and deal in the facts of reality.

Section 6 – *Reverse racism*

The Holocaust killed almost 6 million Jews and 2 million gypsies, mentally ill, retarded, homosexuals and other people Hitler and his Nazis felt were inferior or degenerate in his attempt to "purify" the Germanic/Aryan race in Europe. Does the fact that these groups were victimized give their descendants the right, or entitle them to persecute others if they feel they might be targeted for hatred or discrimination? Does the history of slavery endured by African-Americans make their descendants victims of slavery, even though slavery has been outlawed for centuries and there isn't a black person alive who has personally been held as a slave in America. Subsequent to the abolishment of slavery pursuant to the U.S. Civil War, racial discrimination and "de facto" segregation persisted in many parts of America and African-Americans resorted to civil disobedience to gain the support of the federal government to abolish racial discrimination.

27

With the abolishment of slavery and outlawing of institutionalized racial discrimination and segregation, there isn't a person alive today who can be legally subjected to these inhumane practices. However, there is a phenomenon in society that appears to give an exemption to charges of bigotry and racism to blacks while exaggerating those claims against whites. In addition, individuals from minority groups who express racial hatred, prejudice and racist behaviors appear to be given a pass when directed at each other or against whites.

Does that mean colored people are incapable of racism, and the legal system only applies racial discrimination statutes against whites? This appears to be true even though a high percentage of people from racial minority groups also exhibit ignorant and overt demonstrations of racism, usually as part of their subculture. Racism is racism no matter what is the skin color of the racist. Let's own up to the obvious as confirmed by anonymous Internet bloggers and commenters… at least one third of Americans are haters… it's part of the cultural undertone no matter the racial group. No wonder Americans are experts at fomenting wars and killing people.

Section 7 – *Rights for racial self-determinism*

In the American political and legal system, there are unalienable rights that are guaranteed by the Bill of Rights in the U.S. Constitution, among which are the freedom of speech, freedom of the press and freedom of association… freedom of choice. However, in the practice of these supposed freedoms, restrictions are placed upon the populace to limit their expression. For example,

- Freedom of speech – fully one-third or more of Internet bloggers and commenters engage in hateful speech, name-calling, insults and threats rather than simply to state their opinions. Teachers cannot state their personal beliefs while teaching in the classroom, but only make statements that reflect the educational curriculum, or be subject to administrative actions up to and including forced resignation. Only tenured professors have a modicum degree of "academic freedom" to publish their opinions, and where their writings are found to be offensive to their employing university, its faculty or administrators, they can be censored and steps taken to terminate their employment. Don't use certain words while on board commercial airlines... just uttering the words bomb, gun, hijack or other inflammatory words and phrases subjects the speaker to detention or imprisonment. Get the idea? Politically correct speech is welcomed, but all other opinions carry potential penalties. So much for free speech... another conditional illusion and not a right.

- Freedom of the press – how many journalists have been jailed for their unwillingness to disclose their confidential sources to the government? If a journalist is called to testify before Congress, could they muzzle their response and cite freedom of the press – or must they rely on taking the 5th Amendment to avoid recrimination? Neither can be effective because any journalist, or anyone, can be held in contempt of Congress and jailed indefinitely until they cooperate. So much for freedom of the press. Of course politically correct, sensationalistic, scandalous and celebrity gossip press sells, so that's okay. But a disclosure of the inner workings of the NSA will surely brand one a traitor, and his supporters as accomplices who aides and abets traitors like Edward Snowden and obstruct justice by harboring him. Even with the international drag net out for Snowden for making public confidential government files and the help of another leaker and whistleblower, Julian Assange of Wikileaks, Snowden has become a man without a country, subject to arrests or possible assassination.

- Freedom of association. Not if the government has anything to do with it. Any public or private institution, company or agency who receives government funding, or whose clients receives government funds that are paid for services from such entities is not free to choose their associations based on protected classes such as race, sex, disability, religion, age and soon, sexual-preference. So if you are a white red neck who wants to keep your children exposed only to other white red necks and Aryan supremacists, the government won't permit you to do so if they've decided your child should be bussed to a predominantly black school to create a racial balance. Where in the U.S. Constitution does it state that a racial balance is a government right of mandate? It doesn't, but the courts have twisted legalese to justify anything they want.

- In conclusion, we value pedigree dogs and have a national association to set standards for each breed, but how hypocritical that we won't allow human beings the freedom of choice to decide who they wish to associate with. If we mix all of the races in America, it will soon become a nation of mutts, hybridized individuals without sense of where they came from, of a lost of tradition, identity and heritage. We worry about the rapid lost of biodiversity in nature, and artificial preserves are created to protect the purity of their endangered species. White reproduction rate is by far below that of the non-white population, even with China's one-child policy. If we encourage and force race mixing and its probable consequences (don't forget white slave owners often had bastard children with their slaves), then we limit freedom of association and threaten the continued existence of distinct racial and ethnic groups that left alone without government intervention and mandates, appear totally happy associating with people like themselves who share similar subcultures, values and race.

Section 8 *– Rights against racial persecution and adverse discrimination*

Voluntary racial segregation is a reality reserved to non-white people. Domestics usually live among other Domestics in communities such as East L.A., as Asians tend to live among other Asians in communities such as Monterey Park, while South L.A. comprises black communities, whites live in Canyon Country or Malibu and Iranian Jews live in Beverly Hills. However, should a non-white be able to afford Malibu, there are laws that force white neighbors to accept the residence of non-white homeowners. Where there exist an undercurrent of friction between blacks and Hispanics, there have been episodes where Hispanic gang members have torched homes of blacks who moved into their territories. These are social reactions based on racism, or excluding other races.

There is a difference between voluntary racial association (or for that matter, religious, sexual preference, cultural, etc.) and forced racial discrimination. Voluntary segregation is freedom of association. So if a white family wished to join a white Supremacist group that excludes non-whites, they should be able to do so without government sanctions. Other racial groups do that all the time, and it never becomes a public policy issue when for instance Chinese choose to live among other Chinese in Chinatown and join Chinese family associations. Where adverse discrimination comes in is when, for example, a white family wants to move to Chinatown (which is highly unlikely, for as an illustrative example), and the Chinese neighbors block them from buying a house in Chinatown due to racial discrimination. On the flip side, a Chinese family should be allowed to buy a home in an all white neighborhood if they can afford it, and the white neighbors have a right to exclude the Chinese family from their social association, but don't have a right to keep them from buying the house, or to use any form of intimidation, violence or social harassment to "get 'em outta Dodge."

Section 9 – *Shifting national political spectrum*

The Republicans are back on their heels from its failure to gain a majority in the Senate and inability to elect a GOP President to replace Obama. Political pundits have determined that the shifting political spectrum reflecting greater participation in the voting process by a higher number of racial minorities has tipped the scale toward liberalism versus conservatism. The ultra right wing of the GOP reflecting conservative small town views held by relatively homogenous white Americans stands in marked contrast to the liberal leanings of city folks whose exposure to interracial cooperation in the work place is commonplace for all racial groups, whites, blacks, brown, yellow, red and mixed races.

The primary reason the Tea Party and most GOP politicians are against comprehensive immigration reform that provides a path to citizenship is it permits upwards of 14 million illegal immigrants, of whom over 95% are non-white (not including those lighter skin Hispanics who may otherwise consider themselves white) and more likely to vote for liberal candidates and those from minority groups than for white people. Even were Obama to take the path to citizenship out of the bipartisan Senate compromise bill and instead replace citizenship with an orderly path to obtaining a "green care" or permanent residency without the possibility of citizenship, the House conservatives pressured by Tea Party activists would most likely block that attempt also because it would give the natural born children of green card holders automatic birthright citizenship. It would be possible as a voting block for the natural born citizen children of permanent residents to push for future changes to enfranchise their parents.

Chapter 2 – *Shifting global power distribution and its effect on ethnicity and race*

Capitalism and globalization has created mega wealth and an elite class of billionaires now reflecting people from many nations on all continents. To the elites, race is not their compelling grounds for discrimination in so much as their ownership class separates them from the working classes and the poor. As middle-class income continues to erode from economic stagnation, stock market crashes, recessions, and government monetary policies, the world economic order is less reflective of the traditional hierarchical socioeconomic pyramid and more defined as a bifurcated class construct of the wealthy one percenters versus the rest… a global financially and economically related construction. Where will the American workers fit into the global economic scheme where their jobs are exported and the products they used to manufacture in the USA are imported?

If news reporters were to randomly ask people in different parts of the United States what it means to be American, they'd probably receive a broad range of opinions depending on many factors, including age, race, ethnic heritage, rural versus urban, region of the nation, economic status, education level, occupation, and perhaps even gender. Does being a loyal American simply mean honoring "the flag", and knowing the words to "The Stars Spangled Banner"? Does being American mean the willingness to die to protect our shores, Constitution, citizens, and way of life? Is being an American patriot demonstrated by our insistence on the basic rights to humane treatment, differences in opinion, and religious freedom, which we also encourage around the world? Does being American mean honoring the brilliance of our nation's founders, who rejected their own homelands to courageously fight for their enduring belief in freedom and democracy? Certainly, being American means all of that, and much more. It's no wonder people from all over the world seek refuge, freedom and opportunity in this great land, America.

How should Americans pay back the debt to those who have genuinely cared about each and every life in our country, veterans who fought and died to protect us? Yes, each and every one of them deserved a better life, and they fought to give that to us, to our children, and to our nation and the world. Military families have honored America by contributing their lives and loved ones to protect freedom and our way of life. And for those principles, they died so we may live on as one great nation, America. But as the push toward one global order eliminates national loyalties among the super rich who see the US as just another market for exploitation, nationalism and patriotism is often viewed as an obstacle to free no holds bar capitalism.

But we all know that the world is far from being perfect. Sadly, too many people still suffer in their lives, under the rule of autocratic and oppressive regimes all over the world. How can we, as citizens and residents in this great land, make things better for each other, and people who are suffering from hunger and oppression? Together as Americans, we live together in our communities, go to work, attend schools, and worship side by side, as we strive to live in peace and partnership. But current events remind us that "getting along" is not such an easy thing. Not between nations, and not even between individuals. Why is the world so dangerous and chaotic? Why can't people just respect each other's racial and sexual differences, and the right to live together among each other in communities based upon acceptance, mutual respect and cooperation?

So what does it mean to be an American? Being American is first loving the fact that we have freedom, rights and the rule of law. Sure, it's not perfect because there are almost 300 million Americans living side-by-side, each wanting to get along, but occasionally falling short of that goal. Being American is to be proud of the fundamental philosophical beliefs of our Constitution, and our great opportunities to improve the economic level for anyone who is willing to work hard, save, and contribute to society, regardless of one's class status or cultural background. Being American is about working together for common goals, that of economic prosperity, family unity, community strength, respect for law, and love of life and God. Being American is loving the fact that each and everyone of us has heritages anchored in proud civilizations of the past, as we're all the evolved descendants of past struggles and discoveries, which we have brought together to forge the greatest civilization and nation in the history of human beings, the United States of America.

It's an honor to be American. There has never been in human history a civilization and nation such as ours, the United States of America. Every American has a role to play to make our nation a safe place for children, our families, communities, and for us. Together, we can make good things happen in

America through charity, volunteerism, political engagement, and voting. We can inspire greater trust for our government representatives by helping to build them up, rather than to tear them down. Since 1953, the National Election Study has shown a consistently decline in most Americans' trust of the federal government, a trend that has reversed since the 911 WTC holocaust, but has reverted back to lower trust levels where Congress receives an approval rating of less than 20% from voters. Patriotism is not a core subject taught in schools, and is only popularized by mass media and in pop culture during times of foreign wars where American households send their family members to fight people in distant lands from different religions, races, ethnic groups and beliefs.

Prior to 911, Americans continued to distrust their government, as only 34% expressed trust in the federal government (McIntosh & Parker). Disillusionment with political leaders and dissatisfaction with the way government performs its duties are essential factors that cause distrust of government. However, distrust of government and discontent is not fostering a disregard for the nation's laws, eroding patriotism or discouraging government service, suggesting Americans are frustrated with government rather than angry with it (McIntosh & Parker). Consequently, even though 38% of a *small* segment of those who are most angry at government could see justification for violent acts against the federal government, there is no indication that these attitudes are near a crisis stage to become a threat to our democratic government (McIntosh & Parker).

Even during the height of President Clinton's scandalous charges of adultery and perjury, trust declined only modestly (5%) in public opinion polls, suggesting that distrust of government is more often connected to how people feel about the overall state of the nation (McIntosh & Parker). However, studies also appear to indicate that distrust of political leaders and lack of faith in the political system are principal reasons that the public distrust government. It also appears that cynicism about political leaders and the political system is more crucial to distrust than concerns about the proper role of government, worries about its power and intrusiveness, misgivings about its priorities, or resentment about taxes (McIntosh & Parker).

In addition, the PEW Research Center found in November 1996 that over 60% of survey respondents believed an increase in pessimism about the country's future was due to increasing problems with crime, drugs, and low moral and ethical standards, while perceived level of crime appears to have an opposite correlation on trust, i.e. more murders, less trust (McIntosh & Parker). There is also the potential effect of electoral cynicism and alienation. Academic researchers seek to discover potential causalities in the political culture of our nation to determine the meaning and likely future manifestations of decreasing public trust of our representational democratic system. Does the decline in trust indicate a loss of support for incumbency or for the democratic system? (Luttbeg and Ganz). The current level of political trust has steadily declined since 1964, indicating a steady decline of public trust in government from the 75% level during 1958-64 to recent 20-30% levels (Luttbeg and Ganz), except during the Reagan era when trust rose to the 40% level (Flanigan and Zingale). The issue of "trust to do right" is described by Klosko as the perception of legitimacy and personal benefits. Individuals insist on personal interpretations of the concept of trust which is evidenced by the tendency of voters to trust the politicians that they voted to elect, versus those of the opposing party (Mason).

The relationship between political trust and system stability is thought to be causal by political scientists such as Arthur Miller (Luttbeg and Ganz). The decline of trust in government is thought have a potentially negative effect on system stability; however, no empirical evidence lends credence to the view that democratic governance is threatened by floundering trust in the federal government. Are, as Dr. Miller opined, higher levels of distrust for the political system a precursor of great danger for the American system of government, and are lower trust levels of any significant threat to the status quo? (Luttbeg and Ganz).

In addressing the NES question asked respondents, "Do you trust the federal government to do right?", various independent studies suggest correlations between trust and political obligation (Klosko), the effects of public culture(Mason), justice (Mason), and fairness (Klosko). Other political theorists have advanced causal relationships between levels of trust and variables that include understanding of democracy (Mason), expectations (Kimball), perception of crime, scandals, the state of the economy (Chanley), alienation and presidential performance (Erber & Lau), and incumbency (Parker).

Data from the American National Election Study indicates that Asian-Americans are more likely to have a higher trust in the federal government than African-Americans and whites. A *Chi Square* of (p=0.00) is statistically significant in supporting data that 44% of Asian-Americans, as compared to 28% of whites and blacks trust the federal government to do right "just about always" or "most of the time". Elderly voters in retirement age (65 and older) also tend to have greater trust in government than younger voters, with 37.6% expressing "trust" just about always or most of the time, as compared to 29.4% for ages 18-29, 24.9% for the

30-49 group, and 28.4% for ages 50-64. The results are statistically significant, with a *Chi Sq*uare of (p=0.00) that validates the 8% to 13% difference between voters in retirement age (over 65) as compared to the rest of the population (ANES).

Why do Asian-Americans and those 65 or over appear to trust the federal government to do right, more than other sectors of the population? The fact that upwards of one-third of Asian-American females marry outside their ethnic heritage in the U.S. may suggest that their value for the American people, culture and democracy tends to be generally high, resulting in a higher level of trust for the federal government. In the case of retirees 65 and over, their eligibility for government Social Security benefits may tend to encourage more favorable attitudes toward the federal government, and their regular receipt of monthly checks would certainly tend to favor more trust than distrust. Other potential explanations for the significantly higher level of government trust attributable to the elderly may reflect their greater tendency to have "at-home" lifestyles, where they are affected less by issues of crime and violence than that of the general population who are more socially active and exposed to greater social perils. Asian-Americans may also feel, like the Japanese-Americans felt during World War II, that they have to prove to the larger society that they are loyal Americans, to gain greater mainstream social acceptance.

Political scientists attempt to evaluate the patterns of trust, alienation, and anti-government sentiment with our democracy to ascertain the potential threshold at which respect for the system may plummet below "a point of no return". Consequently, academicians analyze the electoral landscape, demographic patterns, attitudinal change, and political culture to determine if there are clear indicants of verifiable predictors of citizens' political behaviors. Political science research literature and studies have not explained these variances adequately, and any definitive inter-dependencies may be difficult to prove.

Kimball, instead, suggests that citizens appear to make comparisons between what they expect their elected representatives in congress to be like and what they perceive these representatives actually are like, indicating citizens disapprove of Congress when they're not getting the Congress they want (with honest, community-minded members); or because they feel they're getting a Congress they don't want (inhabited by partisan, career-oriented, lawyer legislators). In our two-party competitive system, the political culture encourages and needs both loyalty and dissent. It is the absence of disruptive acts by a substantial portion of society and not the presence of supportive attitudes that is essential for maintaining an established democracy (Flanigan and Zingale). Consequently, it is doubtful that distrust of government alone could be a threat to the American system, an opinion supported by Citrin who felt that distrustful individuals were not ready to repudiate the American form of government (Luttbeg and Ganz). Moreover, Luttbeg and Ganz observed public perception that "government leaders were corrupt and served primarily special interest groups", which lowered trust in government. They observed that "...in general, the public has considerable confidence in the institutions of government, but not much confidence in the individuals charged with operating these institutions."

Anderson observed that "low levels of citizen support can pose serious problems for democratic systems because both their functioning and maintenance are intimately linked with what and how people think about democratic governance, adding, "...alienation from the issues by both major parties of candidates will lead to declining trust in government. We also find evidence that political cynicism is associated with greater approval of anti-government protest..." Prolonged discontent and alienation from the political system many challenge its legitimacy and, ultimately, its very existence. Political participation through the established channels may decrease, and constituents may be tempted to support radical political solutions.

The decline of trust in government is thought have a potentially negative effect on system stability. A causal relationship between political trust and system stability is thought to exist, as observed by notable political scientists such as Arthur Miller (Luttbeg and Ganz), who are among those concerned about the long-term decline in trust levels for our political institutions. This group of theoreticians feel that, "The political culture is a fundamental element of any democratic political system... the values and opinions of the people are the foundation of democracy" (Flanigan and Zingale). Consequently, he opined that higher levels of distrust for the political system is a precursor of "great danger for the American system of government." Miller viewed declining trust as quite serious and an indication that "...the whole system of government is threatened" (Luttbeg and Ganz).

Political scientists are divided on the origins of voter cynicism and dissatisfaction, with some feeling disapproval of both Democratic and Republican policy alternatives causes the most cynicism, while others arguing that it is dissatisfaction with incumbent leaders, rather than their policies, that make people cynical. Political scientist study trust in government because (in theory) it reflects on the stability of a country's government. People who distrust their system of government, who do not view it as legitimate are supposedly more prone to anti-government activities. Research data tend to support this notion of legitimacy, but only as it applies to citizens who display negative personality chronicity, that is, have internalized feelings about particular politicians, and thus may be more likely to legitimize anti-government feelings and actions. When the basic policy alternatives offered by the two major parties or their leaders causes cynicism, this leads to distrust of governmental.

On the contrary, Citrin assures us that political cynics were as likely to be eligible for "good citizenship awards" as their trusting counterparts. Furthermore, Citrin felt that distrustful individuals were not ready to repudiate the American form of government. He compared political systems to baseball teams, with slumps and winning streaks, and what matters most is *winning or losing*, and *not how it plays the game* (Luttbeg and Ganz). Americans continue to play the political game, but in declining numbers that appear to level off above the 50th percentile, except during times of war, when a resurgence of patriotism, electoral participation, and trust in government tend to increase.

Political scientist believe voting adds to stability in America because it convinces citizens that their votes do count. In addition, citizens who participate gain a sense of being integrated into the political system, thus content citizens are not likely to fall victims to demagogues and revolutionaries. Luttbeg and Ganz observed that a majority of the alienated continue to show some faith in democratic government by voting in presidential elections, and though they are less likely to vote than the less alienated, the extremely alienated actually voted more. Flanigan and Zingale summarizes the nonvoting dilemma by stating, "Does the trend suggest that people are satisfied with what government is doing and therefore see no reason to vote? If so, the decline may not be a source of concern. Does the decline mean that people are growing increasingly dissatisfied with their government? If so, is there a "critical threshold" of turnout, below which support for the system crumbles and chaos reigns? Or is declining turnout unrelated to these feelings, assuming they even exist? Since the democracy with the lowest turnout, the United States, has been enduring and stable, turnout may not even be important to democracy."

The real threats to our way of life and system of governance are both internal and external, and have little to do with electoral attitudes toward vote choice per se, and more to do with media manipulation of the public opinion on issues of candidacy, economic outlook, moral issues, and international affairs. In addition, external forces, such as state terrorism, state-sponsored terrorism, or extremist terrorism have shown the potential to disrupt the economic fabric of our nation; however, the strength and resolve of American institutions, government, and the people has prevented a larger economic slowdown. The terrorists' attacks and financial downturn subsequent to 911 demonstrated that one major terrorist incident contributed to increasing the national unemployment rate by an estimated one percent, as over 800,000 additional people lost their jobs during the months immediately following the attack on America. Over a three-month period, the stock market rebounded to its position prior to 911, but the mass layoffs in certain industries, such as those related to air travel, hospitality, and tourism still lingers in severe recession.

What would likely happen to the American economy if two or three such terrorist attacks occurred, perhaps biological or nuclear terrorism that might kill ten times the number of people who lost their lives in the WTC towers and the Pentagon? Argentina is experiencing massive urban rioting after unemployment rates reached 20 percent. In America, unemployment among young adults in the inner cities often exceed 20 percent, contributing to the growth and persistence of a rampant drug and crime culture, founded in violence. Unseen enemies that profit from fear present a greater threat to democracy than low voter turnout or low trust in government could ever cause. A depressed domestic economy, resulting in idle hands and empty stomachs would likely lead to massive public pandemonium, and result in urban warfare.

We need to fear little from citizens who believe in the electoral process, whether their personal candidate choices win or lose. We have more to fear from those citizens who have "chosen" to become disconnected from our democratic system, because they don't feel their participation has any appreciable effect on outcomes of the governing bodies. These will be the first in line for the next series of civil unrest and anti-government activities. With the emergence of multiculturalism as a reality of American culture, "tried and true" homogenous explanations are no longer adequate models to explain underlying public or political sentiment. Questions on the minds of many citizens include whether or not a race war is inevitable, and whether the wealthy are unfairly taking advantage of the system by corrupting our elected officials through special interests lobbying and incidental monetary contributions.

The insider-trading and fraud that lead to Enron's bankruptcy, which rewarded executives while destroying employee pensions, is another example of corruption that causes citizens to be wary and dissatisfied with the job that the federal government is doing, and whether to trust their elected officials and government oversight agencies to do their job in the public's best interest.

Another typical citizen complain is there isn't enough "common sense", and there's too many laws and regulations, resulting in mass confusion. Over 75% of Americans live month to month, and don't have a realistic back-up plan in the event they lose their jobs, and almost everyone at one time or another has technically "broken the law". We may be sitting on a domestic powder keg, whose fuse is tied to the economic health of our nation and communities.

In some respects, we Americans are prisoners of our own desire to be "numero uno", the "top dog", and "second to none". Yet our nation's dismal performance on academic test scores in comparison to other developed nations create a climate of self-denial (the TIMMS cross-national study on student achievement places the U.S. near the bottom as compared to other major industrial democracies). And therein lies our Achilles heel, because our schools are failing to sufficiently impart fundamental education, built around American philosophical and constitutional principles, to our children's generation. Creeping governmental malaise also slowly saps both the trust and confidence of citizens in our system's ability to implement American ideals. The dissonance caused by the disparity between ideals and practice result in greater electoral and popular cynicism that fosters increased distrust and declining support for our political institutions.

Should our educational system and teachers be required to build students' trust and support for the political system? Or is it primarily the job of elected officials, by their speech and actions to arouse and instill public confidence in our system of governance? It's likely citizens would be more trusting if politicians were perceived as being more honest and forthright, but low levels of knowledge of America's Constitutional principles also hinders the maintenance of a healthy level of patriotism, and in some cases may lead to the development of extremist "love it or leave it" types of nationalistic supremacists who encourage intolerance and violence against citizens and symbols of our great democracy. A healthy balance of ethical political behavior and an informed electorate is an essential safeguard for our democracy.

Since WWII, America has had the potential to be a country where everyone who is born has a right to food, shelter, health care, employment, and is guaranteed freedom and peace. But the world has become a far more dangerous place since that time, as the post-cold war era is giving way to the proliferation of extremist nation-states on the verge of attaining nuclear and biological weapons of mass destruction. Many terrorist nation-states sponsor and plan future attacks on America and American interests all over the world. Americans must become better prepared to fight the future battles against terrorism, both globally, and right here on our own homeland soil.

AMERICA'S SECURITY NEEDS CAUSE RACIAL AND ETHNIC PROFILING

Government whistleblower Edward Snowden who stole confidential and secret NSA files and has been branded a traitor was able to get away with thousands of pages of classified data because he is white and didn't fit the racial and ethnic profile of potential spies and terrorists. Let's take a look at the probably security plan in place to deal with potential terrorists and spies. What issues must Homeland Security officials and boots on the ground deal with and how do they go about discovering security risks and threats? What racial and ethnic profiling is used to focus valuable resources on the most probable groups of suspects?

1. Identification of potential terrorists
    a. Who (people who are in sleeper cells, and active in terrorism) are likely Moslems, therefore predominantly from Arab nations such as Saudi Arabia, Iraq and Afghanistan, African countries such as Somalia, African-American such as Black Muslims, Asian from Moslem nations such as Pakistan and Indonesia. Don't bother looking at whites except for anti-government and anti-taxation white Americans who may fit an extremist ideology profile such as the rare domestic terrorist Oklahoma bomber Tim McVeigh. While the Boston bomber brothers appeared white or European, they were ethnic Chechens who are Muslims with hatred toward the U.S.
    b. Where (places potential terrorists meet) such as Mosques, on-line anti-American Muslim sites, Islamic websites and blogs, and other ethnic places where anti-American loyalties likely exist. Don't bother with mainstream Christian or Catholic churches, synagogues or Buddhist temples.
    c. What tactics to use without arousing suspicion and media hyped up stories about racial, religious and ethnic profiling? The NSA phone numbers crunching program PRISM authorized by the Patriot Act permits the random matching of international calls to known or suspected terrorists. While the media and civil libertarians consider the NSA's anonymous phone correlation program as an infringement on American's constitutional privacy rights, no body listens in on any phone calls unless there is probable cause and a court order is

obtained. Of course, there is likely specific targeting of individuals who might fit the potential terrorist profile as previously described.

2. Civil Defense System

    a. Monitoring potential terrorists or their sympathizers who work in various public services and industries, such as airlines, biological, chemical, cyber, nuclear, or genetic fields where weaponization or contamination or sabotage of resources can lead to massive deaths.

    b. Monitoring potential terrorist scouting of targets… non-white people who loiter around and take many photos of potential targets such as

        1) Residential areas near forests that can be set ablazed

        2) Public venues with high population counts such as hi-rise office buildings, stadiums, airports, and train stations

        3) Schools and universities

        4) Infrastructure such as bridges, dams and aquedutes.

        5) Places of employment to disrupt power grid or media towers

The post 911 domestic security programs have greatly expanding the role of the government in monitoring its populace. As more government cameras on the streets are integrated into the face scan database, real and potential terrorists and those who fit a "terrorist profile" may become identifiable to prevent attacks. When people have good reasons to live (love of family, career, nation, and a peace-loving God versus an angry revengeful one), and few or no reasons to die (money problems, religious fanaticism, hatred of government, etc.), then it is highly likely those who desire to live will attempt to be law-abiding and productive citizens of their nations and world.

The fanatical jihad types are obviously twisting their religious doctrine to justify their blatant disregard for human lives. Tim McVey's hatred of our federal government gave him the justification to become a wanton mass murderer without a conscience. John Phillip Walker Lindh, aka Abu Sulayman al-Irlandi, the American Taliban, could not have possibly joined forces with a rogue extremist terrorist group had he received proper and adequate religious and patriotic education from his parents and American public schools.

It's not uncommon for mass murderers to have had incidents in their lives that caused or contributed to the development of their sick perspective on life. No one is born to be a natural mass murderer, and movies that describe the "bad seed" are fictional. It's a stereotype, like stating certain racial groups such as blacks are not as intelligent or are more violent than others, when in fact

42

socioeconomic disparity, poverty, blight and depravity has a greater consequence on behavior than societies would like to admit.

If societies in the world teach love, and not hatred, and the global socioeconomic system permits all people to live relatively free of starvation and oppression, then it's likely the levels of hatred would decrease. But if people see their fathers, mothers, siblings, and children either starve to death, or get blown away in some stupid conflict that serves to settle the power trips of various so-called leaders in certain autocratic nation-states, then the world will continue to be conflictual, and perhaps accelerate circumstances that may lead to a possible nuclear conflict, or human extinction. That's the long-term outcome of the unchecked and continuous build up of weapons of mass destruction by terrorist states and secret terrorist groups, which must stop.

The short-term problem of identifying and neutralizing terrorists who live in many nations requires continued global cooperation and reach, which led by our government, is attempting to tackle and resolve. This war on terrorism must be fought on two fronts; the capture and imprisonment of terrorists, and capturing the hearts and minds of our citizens and potential enemies. Improving economic conditions so people don't starve and join terrorist breeding camps takes away terrorists' opportunities to entice recruits with false promises, brainwashing propaganda, and food filled with hatred for the United States of America. It's only common sense, that if a man is starving, and his family is starving, and the only way to live is to join some extremist group to get food and a feeling of self-respect, what person in that desperate state of mind might not seriously consider joining any terrorist group? But if we think that terrorism can't be prevented, then we might as well give up and surrender our liberty, freedoms and our nation to all the crazy people. The vast majority of Americans and free people in the world won't give up in our fight against terrorism, because we can't. We have no other choice than to defeat terrorism in its present form, to defeat it at its roots, and to alter its seeds of hatred.

Our government is doing the best it can in this new era of uncertainty. We should give our elected officials, military and bureaucrats our support, and instead of making negative criticisms, we should advance positive suggestions. So how can we guard against the thousands and thousands of potential terrorist scenarios and conspiracies that might or might not happen in the future? We all need to form tighter communities, and be aware of our environments. We can all try to do things that would likely make the future brighter for our loved ones, communities, nation, the world, and ourselves. Individually, we may seem insignificant in comparison to all the powerful people and forces in the world, but collectively and spiritually, all of our souls and feelings do in some way change the potential outcomes of unfolding future scenarios. And should bad things still happen (eventually bad things always do find a way to surface), we could feel that in our own little ways, we tried our best to be descent human beings. It's a historical fact that bad things happen in the world from time to time, but fortunately, much more good things happen on a regular basis.

It's very easy to judge others if we haven't walked in their shoes, and think that we will never have to walk in their shoes. Most Arabs who are poor and believe in Islam will never turn out to be terrorists and use the jihad as an excuse to attack and kill innocent people. But, even here at home in America, poverty breeds violence, gangs, crime, and hatred. So why wouldn't poverty become a breeding ground for violence anywhere else? Solutions do exist, but it requires sustained commitment, time, and money. And most importantly, it takes positive examples, education, mentoring, and guidance. When people are fulfilled and relatively happy and connected in their lives, they don't think to do evil things. But people like the uni-bomber and bin laden have something wrong in their lives, that makes them hate so much. These types of people, if we can even call them that, are devoid of emotional and spiritual conscience or love of humanity, and they must be caught and locked up so they can't infect others, especially the impressionable young.

The U.S. is the leader and broker of international coalitions from the U.N., to NATO, to "Desert Storm", to the "war on terrorism." If any nation can police the world and push historical antagonists into a peace settlement in the Middle East, it would most likely be the U.S., because it is the hegemon, the most powerful nation in the history of the world, both militarily and economically. During WW2, the U.S. government earned its preeminence by proving it had the ability to engender patriotism and unquestioned support of government policies by its citizens during times of crisis. Most nations of the world are beholden to the U.S. for one thing or another, for American cash, industry, technology, liberation, modernization... something. Since the international community owes the U.S. so much, it owes America its full support and cooperation.

The bottom line is economic power, coupled with a powerful military, driven by technology, and supported by a patriotic citizenry, allows the U.S. to utilize various strategies to carry out policies that benefit those groups of elite domestic actors who exert the greatest influence on our government. When international situations threaten American hegemony, the U.S. government steps in to protect

44

U.S. corporate interests and to protect the American economy, whether the cause of disequilibria is oil prices, the nuclear arms race, or terrorism. Benefits that the American power elite derives from the international system usually trickles down to the American masses, who as a group still enjoys one of the highest per capita incomes in the world (however, as the U.S. economy becomes more bifurcated, the poor is increasingly taking on some of the attributes typically ascribed to Third World populations).

Nations around the world can receive adequate assistance when they give in to playing the economic game by the international rules that has been developed and brokered by the United States of America, which insures American dominance and hegemony. We are very lucky to be Americans, because it's always much better to be on the winning side than anywhere else. And as citizens, we have much we collectively owe to the brave soldiers who have fought on foreign battlefields, to prevent our homeland from becoming a future battlefield. Despite all of our faults as a culture, our imperfect government and legal system, and criticisms regarding our over consumptive superficial lifestyles, America remains the most powerful nation in the history of planet Earth, and for good reasons. America continues to set high standards for all people who believe in freedom, justice, and equal opportunity. The Homeland Security Act was quickly enacted to protect us, and while some civil liberties have been cut back, American is still by far the "land of the free, and the home of the brave." It's far better to be relatively free and alive, than to be anarchically free, and dead. We all must make our temporary sacrifices, and until the world is relatively safe again for the citizens of our planet, we should trust our government to do the best job that they can for us. Fighting an invisible enemy cannot possibly be an easy job.

American power comes from the fact that the world owes the U.S. so much, most of which is still outstanding debt, and the fact that real patriots love our nation so much that they are willing to put their lives in harms way, time and time again. Those nations who are stupid enough to bite the hand that feeds them (like several countries our military has helped to free in the past), then they should not receive an invitation to share in the future development of our world. There can only be long-lasting peace among the neighborhoods, as long as U.S. interests aren't threatened, and Americans are safe to travel to any place in the world.

American residents enjoy all the blessings and opportunities we have in America... it's at least 1000 times better than living in Afghanistan. Most Islamic regimes are not tolerant of other religions, a remarkable right that is guaranteed by our U.S. Constitution. In fact, many Islamic states follow the Nazi philosophy of rounding up people who don't believe like them, then subjecting them to kangaroo trials, then executing them. American soldiers have risked their lives to protect American Christians from intolerance by saving our American missionaries from the Taliban. We should not accept the legitimacy of any regime that executes innocent people solely on account of their personal religious beliefs. Any nation, whether Islamic or whatever who practices religious fascism, and have anti-Christian or anti-Semitic laws and customs, should not benefit from U.S. trade or protection, because one of the primary founding principles of this land, America, was religious freedom.

America is the world's torch holder of religious freedom, and here, we don't arrest Moslems and execute them on account of their belief in Islam... we arrest them only if they are suspected of crimes or terrorist activities. Here in America, people from all world religions can live side by side in peace, without government persecution or harassment (a few nuts may be guilty, but not our laws, government, and culture). There are protections written into the Constitution and Congress has passed many laws to insure equal rights and equitable treatment under the law. Blacks, whites, Hispanics, Asians, Native Americas, Jews, Arabs, mix-race individuals, the young, the old, the disabled, and alternative lifestyle practitioners all enjoy the same unalienable rights. God bless America and our countless unsung heroes from shore to shore, and all who risk their lives daily on foreign soil and at home, so we may remain prosperous and free to worship who we want. All Americans should never forget the debt we owe to all those brave souls who have died to keep America the land of the free.

References:

ANES. *American national elections study.* http://sda.berkeley.edu:7502

Chanley, Virginia A., Rudolph, Thomas A., and Rahn, Wendy M. (2000). *The origins and consequences of public trust in government: A time series analysis.* Public Opinion Quarterly, Vol 64, pp. 239-256.

Erber, Ralph, and Lau, Richard R. (Feb. 1990). *Political cynicism revisted: An information-processing reconciliation of policy-based and incumbency-based interpretations of changes in trust in government.* **American Journal of Political Science**, Vol 34, No. 1, pp. 236-253.

Flanigan, William and Zingale, Nancy H. (1998). *Political behavior of the American electorate* 9th edition. Congressional Quarterly, Incorporated.

Kimball, David C., and Patterson, Samuel C. (1997). *Living up to expectations: public attitudes toward Congress.* The Journal of Politics, Vol 59, No. 3, pp. 701-728.

Klosko, George (1992). *The principle of fairness and political obligation.* Lanham, MD: Rowman & Littlefield Publishers, Inc.

Luttbeg, Norman R., and Ganz, Michael M. (1994). *American electoral behavior, 1952-1992*, 2nd edition, Best Peacock, F. E. Publishers, Incorporated.

Mason, Andrew (1993). *Maintaining political disagreement.* NY: Cambridge University Press.

McIntosh, Mary, and Parker, Kimberly (2001). *Deconstructing distrust. How Americans view government.* Princeton, NJ: The Pew Research Center For The People & The Press.

Parker, Suzanne L., and Parker, Glenn R. (May 1993). *Why do we trust our congressman?* The Journal of Politics, Vol. 55, No. 2, pp 442-453.

A moral dilemma for a representational democracy such as the United States is the actual or potential influence on political policies by the collusion of a power elite comprised of military, bureaucratic, corporate, and political leaders. This section addresses three primary issues that impact the bureaucratic ethics in the Military-Industrial Complex (MIC) have on America and its relationship to causing false flag wars against people of color all over the world. President Dwight Eisenhower who was a 6 star Commanding General during WW2 stated his concern that the powerful military industrial machine could bear undue influence in the halls of power to cause our military to interdict in foreign wars that are manufactured for corporate profits, and paid for by the blood of our brave troops in harms way and untold numbers of the innocent we demonize as enemies to justify the escapades of war and to create a jingoistic war fervor among the general population to pressure lawmakers with patriotic justification for war. We must ask some basic questions on the desirability to send our families to fight and kill people in the underdeveloped and undeveloped 3rd world nations populated by non-whites. Is warfare becoming more a surreptitious population control and resource accumulation strategy designed to create corporate profits for the war industry? Isn't killing colored people under false pretenses the worse form of racism, even more insidious than the Manifest Destiny moral mandate doctrine derived by certain white men directly from God? Let's ask some basic questions before allowing our leaders to take our patriotic families to war.

1) Does the close relationships within the Military-Industrial Complex create a tempting environment for corruption?

2)   Does collusion exist between elite military brass, politicians, and
industrialists to use procurement contracts and military bases as political
payoffs for corporate profits?

3)   Does the undue influence of the MIC alter foreign policy decision-making to
create or support global conflicts that require military interventions, which
result in profit to corporations and retired military brass?

Discussion

**1.   Does the close relationships within the Military-Industrial Complex
create a tempting environment for corruption?**

The institutionalized network of an extensive military bureaucracy and large
sweetheart defense contractors creates a tempting environment for potential
unethical practices and mismanagement in contracts and procurement.
Industrialists and military leaders have viewed their interests as mutual, where the
armed forces bureaucracy granted special favors, increased military budgets,
financed research, and encouraged industrial monopoly with little incentive to
restraint profits in preferred business sectors (Koistinen,1980: 832). The MIC is a
unique creature when compared to ethical safeguards that are part of standard
governmental practices. Unless the military sat in on corporate decisions, they
would not be sure that their programs would be carried out; and unless corporate
executives knew something of the war plans, they could not plan war production.
As a result, the very structure of military economics created a convenient merging
of interest and political collusion among CEOs seeking economic gain, and military
chiefs seeking equipment to fight wars (Pursell, 1972: 67).

Contracts have become one of the most common and lucrative sources of
corruption in government. Incentives for private contractors to engage in bribery,
kickbacks, and pay offs obviously exist, and corruption is inevitable if public
officials in charge of the contracting process are sufficiently self-interested, bold,
and lack direct accountability (Benson, 1998: 45). As of February 1969, some

2,072 retired military officers at or above the rank of colonel or Navy captain were employed by 100 defense contractors, and the 10 largest companies employed 1,065 retired officers (Pursell, 1972: 254). Less than 12% of military contracts are awarded on a formally advertised competitive bid basis. The potential for major abuse is present because almost 90 percent of all military contracts are negotiated, but a very high proportion of them are negotiated with only one or two contractors (Pursell, 1972: 257). The bulk of the defense budget goes for military purposes, and not for military pay, at the same time 100 companies "earn" 67 percent of defense contract dollars because cost overruns are normal, and major military weapon systems usually exceed their initial estimates by 100 to 200 percent (Pursell, 1972: 258).

Historians of the military-industrial complex have often noted its massive waste that occurs at every level and location where military contracts are involved. In its efforts to revive the battered private ship-building industry, the metropolitan-military complex was already laying the strategy for shielding the institution of defense spending from normal cost accounting practices (Lotchin, 1970:1006). In one instance, the Navy had requested Electric Boat to drill a one-and-a-half-inch hole in radiation shielding boxes on the Trident submarines, and the company notified the navy that the change would cost $1,000 for each hole drilled. In another case, the navy requested a wire rope to be added to each of the Trident submarine's hatches to secure them in the open position. The wire ropes could not have cost more than $5 each to fabricate. But the shipyard informed the government that each wire rope would cost $1,400, and in addition, a two week delay charge, which could reach $100,000 (Tyler, 1986: 252).

The reports of gross overcharges and malpractice have continued unabated, whether as $400 paid for a claw hammer, $7,622 for a coffee maker, or standard work hours billed at over $6,000/hr. That's a high price to pay for military equipment that oftentimes amounts to junk, as from 20 to 30 percent of Navy air-to-air missiles are reported to be unusable due to their inaccuracy (Ullmann, 1985:19). Insufficient scientific and technological expertise, and theoretical knowledge among the military ranks, permit defense contractors to overprice military hardware, justified by "military standards". Even during peacetime, when defense contractors are expected to convert to building consumer products instead of war machines, picking suitable new products is complicated by the internal inefficiencies and routine waste of military firms, and a general lack of marketing skills for non-military products that are not already being adequately supplied someone else (Dumas, 1995: 309-310). Consequently, defense contractors are faced with the dilemma of either attempting to compete in new unfamiliar waters where they don't have any built-in advantages, or they find war markets for their products in other parts of the world.

Clifford (1990: 163) stated, "the bureaucratic politics perspective suggests internal struggles over policy can consume so much time and attention that dealing effectively with external realities become secondary", and as a result, insufficient attention is given to ethical measures. The Department of Defense (DOD) has an oversight system that essentially transfers wealth to influential defense contractors by imposing large penalties primarily on small contractors, while fines against large corporations are relatively small, even though a disproportionate majority of fraud cases involve large firms (Karpoff, 1999: 814). The top 100 contractors have smaller losses in market value than unranked contractors (Karpoff, 1999: 830). Without substantial punishments being meted out, or at least the potential for large penalties, the incentive for ethnical conduct is minimize, as the opportunities for corruption remain significant.

2.   Does collusion exist between elite military brass, politicians, and industrialists to use procurement contracts and military bases as political payoffs and for corporate profits?

To fully understand the criticisms against the MIC, one must begin with a long standing distrust of profits, and the concern over economic motives in warfare. The general distrust of businessmen and the broad economic motives in warfare are historical facts. Criticisms of military-industrial relations are set against public taxpayers' concern with the price, equality, and delivery of military supplies to the government (Moldander, 1976: 59).

An iron triangle of special interests, congressional subcommittees, and media hype is designed to influence public policies that may be against the public's best interests (Petersen, 1990: 538). Congress has shaped government policies, and politicians have organized Congress in a manner to insure their own re-election, with the help of special interests (Petersen, 1990: 543). Consequently, the private and special interests of entrenched defense contractors lobby to gain the governmental seal of approval. This unique buyer-seller relationship, which is contrary to conventional economic standards, lies at the foundation of the military-industrial complex and the power structures that it generates. The MIC is not so much a conspiracy between the "merchants of death" and a group of warmongering generals, but a natural coalition of interest groups with an economic, political, or professional stake in defense spending (Pursell, 1972: 85).

In the example of the San Francisco-based MIC, the leading city newspapers and the Bay Cities Naval Affairs Committee mounted campaigns for opening a naval base. Retired and active military men spoke through the media for greater defense spending, as a son of the President and San Francisco congressmen sponsored so many projects in the House of Representatives, that its Naval Affairs Committee became "the most important committee, from the standpoint of local interest" (Lotchin, 1970: 1005). As evidenced from the levels of defense spending, they peaked during times of conflict, including WW2, the Korean War, the Cuban Missile Crisis, and the Vietnam War (Gansler, 1980: 12). The United States decided that, even in crisis periods, it wanted both "guns and butter." The civilian sector would not be mobilized to produce military goods in a crisis period; instead, military crises would be met from within the defense industry (Gansler, 1980: 13).

In 1987, Department of Defense awarded $133.26 billion in contracts, of which $96.8 billion was reaped as corporate profits, equal to a profit margin of almost 73 percent. This compares to corporate bond yields on average of 9.28 percent for the same year (Mintz, 1992: 89). The annual corporate profits for the ten largest defense contractors increased from an estimated $300 million in 1948 to almost $3.5 billion by 1988, a 11,670 per cent increase in 40 years, or averaging 29 percent per year increase in profits compared to the previous year (Mintz, 1992: 91). Post WW2 military spending acted to stimulate the economy where private demand was insufficient for sustained expansion, and was preferred by industry instead of spending on social programs due to the greater profitability of capitalism (Reich, 1972: 296). Armaments become rapidly consumed or obsolete, resulting in retooling of existing production, and creating a bottomless pit for new technologies and highly specific improved weaponry (Reich, 1972:298).

The most significant factor contributing to congressional votes on defense spending was constituency opinion, with every one-point change in average opinion translating to an estimated change in appropriations of almost $13 billion in the same direction (Dumas, 1995: 237). Baldwin (1967: 103) charged that military bases are located, and contracts placed in certain states in order to win the favor of influential congressmen; that contractors and politicians are able to reverse or delay decisions to cut back or cancel programs; that contracts are awarded to reward supporters of the political party in power and to punish its opponents; that "insiders" are in a position to get awards for their clients through "influence peddling"; that procurement is unduly influenced by a host of retired military officers who are either on the payrolls of major contractors or lobbying for the industry in Washington; and that a more insidious pressure is put on active procurement officials by tempting them with lush positions in private industry after retirement. One piece of objective evidence suggests a lack of power or incentive of the bureaucracy assigned to oversee the MIC, as persistent efforts to eliminate provisions for renegotiating "excessive" profits on defense contracts have been doomed to failure (Baldwin, 1967: 105).

Congressional "Add-ons" in FY 1999 that were military expenditures beyond what the Pentagon asked for is another method that politicians use to bolster their positions in their home districts (Hartung, 1998). Following is a very brief list of prominent politicians and the defense budget riders that they sponsored during FY 1999.

1. Senate Majority Leader Trent Lott, Mississippi for $1.5 billion and $94 million for a Marine helicopter and Space-based laser, respectively.

2. House Speaker Newt Gingrich, Georgia for $397 million + over a $billion in operating expenses over the next six years for 7 C-130Js planes.

3. Rep. Norm Dicks (D-WA), Washington for $86 million for B-2 production support.

4. Rep. John Murtha (D-PA), Rep. Joseph Mcdade (R-PA), Rep. Curt Weldon (R-PA), Pennsylvania for $25 million and $78 million for the Q-70 radar.

5. Sen. Daniel Inouye (D-Hawaii), Hawaii for $258 million for 31 separate projects.

6. Sen. Ted Stevens (R-Alaska), also chair of the Senate Appropriations Committee and defense subcommittee Alaska $1.9 million various projects.

According to Hartung (1998), spreading Pentagon contracts around to the districts of powerful legislators has been a routine practice for decades, but defense budget politics have taken a unique twist in the 1990s. When the Republicans took control of both Houses of Congress in 1994, Congress added billions to the Pentagon budget every year beyond what the Department of Defense requested. This was a sharp reversal from the Reagan years, when liberals in Congress consistently attempted to slice a few billion off from the President's Pentagon budget request. According to the nonpartisan Center for Strategic and Budgetary Assessments, Congress added a total of roughly $20 billion to the Pentagon budget during Fiscal Years 1996-1998. Despite cries from the military and Pentagon budget hawks regarding the "readiness crisis" that had weakened U.S. fighting forces, three-quarters of this $20 billion windfall was earmarked for weapons projects that benefited major defense contractors, and not for maintenance, training, pay, or other items that would improve the safety and quality of life of military personnel.

The add-on game is designed to increase the revenues of major contractors by extending the production life of weapons systems that the Pentagon wants to terminate. The payback for legislators is twofold, as they receive hundreds of thousands of dollars in campaign contributions from the contractors, and they also get to claim credit for high-profile, job-producing weapons projects in their districts. This self-serving process wastes billions of dollars in taxpayer funds that could be put to more productive domestic uses. Equally alarmingly, this circular practice reduces national security by distorting the spending patterns within the Pentagon budget.

Hartung (1998) observed that the C-130 add-on is another example of "the waste that keeps on wasting." Congress had been buying them at such a rapid pace, that since 1991, the Air Force had been forced to retire many perfectly usable C-130Es with more than a dozen years of useful life left. And because Congress doesn't budget funds to operate the extra C-130s, the Pentagon will have to come up with over $1 billion to maintain the unrequested C-130s over a six year period, and redirect funds which will deplete allocations for pay, training, or other "readiness accounts" of the sort that the Joint Chiefs of Staff have claimed continue to be seriously under funded.

In addition to joining with key legislators to insert specific items into the Pentagon budget, companies like Lockheed Martin are also actively engaged in the business of shaping U.S. foreign and military policies to meet their needs. This more devious form of lobbying can involve changing the terms under which major contractors are reimbursed, such as the "payoffs for layoffs" subsidies for defense industry mergers; creating billions of dollars of new grants and government-guaranteed loans to support the export of U.S. weaponry; or lifting longstanding arms control curbs like the ban on the sale of advanced combat aircraft to Latin America (Hartung, 1998). Defense contractors have been heavily in favor of controversial programs or policies that stand to benefit them. Several examples of this type of lobbying are the National Missile Defense program, its Star Wars predecessor, and NATO expansion, which have received on average an extra $1 billion per year as a result of lobbying by Pentagon contractors and conservative research and advocacy groups. The companies which benefited most from such military expansion programs included the likes of Lockheed Martin, Boeing, and Textron that view expansion as a golden opportunity to open up a new, government-approved, tax-payer-subsidized markets for their products (Hartung, 1998).

Hartung (1998) pointed to examples of specific industry lobbying campaigns to illustrate how the Big Three arms producers have used their political clout, which include peddling weapons abroad, lifting the Latin Arms Ban, and promoting NATO expansion. As the Reagan weapons buying binge of the 1980s began to wind down, U.S. weapons manufacturers began to focus more attention on foreign markets as a way to maintain their profit margins. Since foreign sales often entail the transferring of more "mature" technologies in which the bugs have been worked out of the production process, and because the research, development, and initial production runs on the system have been paid for by U.S. taxpayers, exporting weapons are often more profitable than sales of weaponry to the Pentagon. This strategy for obtaining higher profits has driven major weapons producing companies to focus efforts on increasing exports. U.S. companies have benefited the most, cornering 40-50% of the total global arms market during the 1990s.

Having obtained market dominance, companies like Lockheed Martin and Boeing have discovered that an effective way to expand their exports beyond current levels is to change U.S. government policy. Hartung contends that the changes wanted by the MIC involve either opening up new markets, by eliminating existing restrictions based on the human rights or proliferation record of potential recipient states, or through new government subsidies to be used to create more "cash paying customers" in the form of foreign customers that use U.S. taxpayer supplied "aid" in the form of grants and loans to buy U.S. weapons.

3.   **Does the undue influence of the military-industrial complex alter foreign policy decision-making to create or support global conflicts that require military interventions that result in profit to corporations and retired military brass?**

The military's primary role is to protect its nation's citizens and residents from external threat. Control and influence by corporate interests exert capitalistic motives that displaces the best interest of the people, as defense profits are often decisions made without regards to morality or ethics. The period since World War II has been dominated by the ascendance of corporate and military elites to positions of institutional power. These "commanding heights" allow them to exercise control over the trends of the business cycle and international relations (Pursell, 1972: 59). As financial investments followed international trade, increasing investments abroad resulted in expanding the U.S. role in world affairs, justifying a larger navy (Baack, 1985: 372).

In his farewell speech in 1960, President Eisenhower warned against the "conjunction of an immense military establishment and a large arms industry" that could influence the economic, political, and even spiritual life in every city, every state house, and every office of the federal government. By the time Eisenhower left office, the aircraft, munitions, and scientific facilities built during WW2 were so interwoven into the national economy that a disengagement from permanent war production was next to impossible (Albrecht, 1995: 225). Eisenhower warned that the "conjunction" of an immense military establishment and a large arms industry had serious implications and potential consequences. He advised Americans to guard against the acquisition of unwarranted influence, whether sought or unsought, by the military-industrial complex as the potential for the disastrous rise of misplaced power exists and would persist (Albrecht, 1995: 239).

The conjoining of large corporations with the military bureaucracy has created an environment that blurs the ethical line in government. Various examples of questionable ethical arrangements within the MIC include former military brass working for industries they once contracted with, or working in departments that decide on military contracts. Most disturbing is the underlying question, whether foreign affairs are manipulated to create conflicts that result in financial benefits to the MIC? Does the profit motive become the primary motivation to create global conflict, violence and war? Why did the United States assume the role of the world's super cop, causing it to be involved in various foreign wars each decade? Subsequent to WW2 of the 1940's, the U.S. fought the Korean War in the 1950's, followed by the Vietnam War in the 1960's, then the Cold War "arms race" against the Soviets during the '70s, leading to escalating extensive military interventions in Latin America (Nicaragua, Panama, Grenada, etc.) in the '80s, and Desert Storm in 1991.

Thousands of industrialists from the nation's largest corporations, most of whom had benefited from wartime production, guided and assisted the government to help introduce modern business techniques into military operations, and familiarize themselves with military procurement and planning methods (Koistinen, 1970: 826). Often, representatives of trade associations and corporate executives were, or became reserve officers assigned to the military bureaucracy, who then assisted in drafting procurement and mobilization plans that furthered the cooperative relationships between the military and business sectors (Koistinen, 1970: 827). Koistinen (1970: 819) observed that during both World Wars, federal agencies that were largely controlled by industry and the military regulated the economy, and these relationships continued in place into modern times.

Government is primarily a "top-down" process, where elite consensus trickles down to mass public opinion, because the public is easily manipulated by political leaders and the press due to low levels of public knowledge of issues (Reiss-Kappen, 1991: 481). Public opinion and societal groups may influence policy-making by narrowing the range of options available to politicians by influencing the coalition-building processes among the elite bureaucrats or actors within the government (Reiss-Kappen, 1991: 482). Support by mass public opinion appears to be essential for public interests groups and other actors to influence policy decisions (Reiss- Kappen, 1991: 510), but support for the MIC can take on an even more surreptitious form. Can a president, seeking to respond to public preferences or to manipulate public opinion, skillful use conflicts in the international arena, and manipulate mass media to promote foreign policy? (Dumas, 1995: 247). The contingent nature of popular support of political positions generated by war was reflected in the instability of opinion poll trends. One solution to the fleeting quality of crises might be to direct and organize a series of crises, which Patriots Sr. did in fact do (Dumas, 1995: 250), resulting in higher public approval ratings and more profit for the MIC.

Now, with the new millennium, we have begun the protracted "War on

Terrorism" in Afghanistan, with budget approval for over 3,000 advanced tactical jet fighters to be on line by the year 2008, in time for the Olympics scheduled for China. What war do we plan to fight in the year 2010, in the next decade? Perhaps it'll be a war for world domination, or against an extraterrestrial invasion fleet. A clear pattern of major warfare each decade has become apparent, and we need a new enemy each decade to justify enormous military expenditures. Armament firms have been active in fomenting war scares, and in persuading their own countries to adopt warlike policies to increase their weapons profits, and disseminating false reports concerning the military and naval expenditures of various countries in order to stimulate armament expenditures (Molander, 1976: 61). The legitimate need for national defense has served to justify the existence of MICs, as we must be ready at all times for unpredictable events that lurk in the international relations arena. It's no wonder the world remains a hotbed of violence and warfare between contesting factions, as the MIC may have a hidden hand in stirring up international conflicts to create new markets for their wares.

Case Study:

"Operation Enduring Freedom", the U.S.-led "War Against Terrorism"

The public's ability to play a serious and continuous role in foreign policy is limited by its lack of information. At the beginning of conflicts, a surge of patriotism sweeps the country. Threats or perceived foreign police crises are a major fuel for defense budget escalation (Dumas, 1995: 242). Is there, then, a military-industrial complex which prevents peace? Criticism can be additionally made that not only does American society contain a ruling military-industrial complex, but that American society *is* a military-industrial complex (Pursell, 1972: 78-79).

Civilian control of the military has been a long-standing assumption in American history; however, following World War II, the erosion of civilian supremacy was a significant concern of social critics, who saw a small and unified ruling elite controlling the means of resource and power allocation in American society. "Warlords" or top military officers are integral members of the ruling elite, along with elites coming from the pinnacles of the corporate and political bureaucracies (Moskos, 1976: 56). The successful conduct of a military campaign now depends upon industrial supremacy. As a consequence, the armed forces of a nation and its industrial power have become one and inseparable, and therefore unified leadership of both is not only logical but also inescapable (Baumgartner, 1970: 177).

In light of the realities created by the MIC, is it possible that international terrorists are playing right into the hands of corporate profiteers? Immediately after the WTC terrorists attacks on September 11th, the federal bureaucracy and our nation's political leaders rolled into action. With the support of ninety percent of Americans who were still reeling from the shock of the horrific events, the government went on a spending spree, raiding Social Security funds, and placing the nation back on the track of deficit spending. Fifty billion dollars for NYC relief, $200 billion for the advanced technology Joint Attack Fighter (expected to exceed a half trillion dollars by 2008), and whatever it may cost to press the projected decade long war on terrorism, wherever it may lead us, as there remains plenty of "terrorist states" for us to attack after we're done in Afghanistan. According to Secretary of Defense Donald Rumsfeld, the official list of terrorist states include Iraq, Iran, Syria, Lybia, and Cuba, yet over three-fourths of the suicidal terrorists who committed the atrocities of 9-11 were Saudi or Egyptian nationals, our allies. There would have been even more serious ramifications had the 9-11 terrorists been citizens of "terrorist states", in which case the U.S. may have found it convenient to return to Iraq to "finish the job elder Bush had started", and to expand the war effort to other Arab countries.

In any case, the major actors in the MIC have greatly benefited from this latest decade long war on terrorism. Patriots Jr. enjoys the highest rating of any living president, including that of his father, former-Patriots Sr. The military enjoys increased budgetary allocations, and the "intelligence" community has been given permission to "take off the gloves" and to use unsavory strategies to obtain foreign intelligence. The big defense contractors need to manufacture more smart munitions, and propose more technologically advanced systems to carry out our fight to protect our borders and citizens from foreign aggression. Naturally, no one will complain if they make enormous profits in executing that charge. After all, it would be terribly unpatriotic to complain about all our government is doing to protect American citizens. And with the Homeland Security Act of 2001, a set of 200 hastily passed pages of somewhat repressive laws, that may not stand up to Constitutional challenges later if the terrorist threat subsides, we have it on good account that privacy and freedom of speech rights may be targeted for repeal, if not constitutionally, then certainly de facto. But who wants to appear unpatriotic?

Conclusions

Coffman (1984: 16) sets out the idea of relating the military factor in our national public affairs; that of developing weapons, strategic and tactical progress, manpower allocation, and economic policies, with civil history. He thought to show the significance and impact of military institutions and its development of political initiatives, observing that power tends to corrupt, and absolute power corrupts absolutely. American power is no exception, and clearly it has been used for good purposes and bad in terms of liberty, democracy, and human rights. Many will argue that American power is less likely to be misused or corrupted than the power of any other major government. They will point to the reason that because American leaders and decision makers are the products of their culture, they are themselves generally committed to liberal and democratic values (Huntington, 1982: 31). The question arises, to what degree are politicians who are wed to the MIC committed to ethical values engendered by our constitutional democracy? Certainly, the profit motive has some persuasive qualities to influence policy.

In 1965, the U.S. Comptroller General highlighted the following

61

characteristics of the defense contract system before a congressional committee, summarizing the faults, which were:

1.   Excessive prices in relation to available pricing information

2.   Acceptance and payment by the government for defective equipment

3.   Charges to the government for costs applicable to contractors' commercial work

4.   Contractors' use of government-owned facilities for commercial work for extended periods without payment of rent to the government

5.   Duplicate billings to the government

6.   Unreasonable or excessive costs, and

7.   Excessive progress payments held by contractors without payment of interest thereof (Purcell, 1972: 85-86).

The conjunction of an immense military establishment and a large arms industry has its influence on the economic and political aspects of every city, state, and office of the federal government. We must guard against the acquisition of unwarranted influence, whether sought or unsought, by the military-industrial complex (Pursell, 1972: 206-207). There are several major areas that must be examined in the MIC's super bureaucracy, that stretch from the halls of Congress and the Presidential Office, to the Pentagon and executive suites of major corporations. Some of these areas need greater accountability, control, and ethical reform to remove the corruptive opportunities and temptation; however, it's not likely much if anything will be done soon, if ever.

1.   Internal management problems due to complexity and size

2.   Uncertain future deployment

3.   Inter-services conflicts and rivalry regarding role, mission, and funding

4.   Need to purchase expensive equipment without market constraints

5.   Localization pressures to locate facilities as political constituency payoffs

6.   Military budget containing largest "discretionary" items in the federal budget

7. Conflicts of interest between public power, clientelism, and private interest

8. Political payoff in the form of campaign contributions

9. Interagency problems due to large decentralized, competitive, and complex bureaucracy

10. Greater opportunities for stakeholder benefits; business and employees

11. Lack of legislative or bureaucratic transparency due to national security

12. Increasing concentration of power to political and corporate elites

The military industrial firm is the chosen instrument of military production, but it has unique characteristics in its managerial organization, in the risks from which it is protected, and in the manner in which society has chosen to sustain and almost encourage its inefficiencies and dysfunctions (Ullmann, 1985: 12). The close, continuing relationship between the DOD and its major suppliers is resulting in the convergence between the two, which is blurring and reducing much of the distinction between public and private activities, which has been an important dichotomy in the American economy (Ullmann, 1985: 13).

The Military-Industrial Complex is built upon stakeholder interests in budgetary share for research and development, and equipment purchases, with large flexible discretionary items in military budgets to ensure loyalty from the industrial sector, politicians, and the career military.

The government sponsored and approved structure of the MIC network creates legitimacy, as the structure gathers regulators, executives, and politicians who have complementary roles, and places them in closed door dealings and secret budgets to minimize public scrutiny, and to avert public insecurities about future uncertainties. At the same time, the United States is becoming increasingly dependent on foreign supply of a broad range of industrial technologies, all with military significance (Sandholtz, 1992: 13), and is constrained by emerging industrial weakness and a declining ability to ensure adequate domestic markets in return for the MIC's compliance with U.S. foreign policy (Sandholtz, 1992: 198).

This uncertainty drives the MIC to seek foreign policies that will ensure its continued profitability.

Bureaucratic work causes people to displace, while at work, the moralities they might hold outside the workplace or that they might adhere to privately. Instead, people follow the prevailing perceived morality of their immediate organizational situation. Cowton (1998: 44) explains that what is right in the work environment is what the guy above wants from you. That's what morality is in the corporate setting. He goes on to state, "Management is rooted fundamentally in power and politics, and the exercise of power attracts its fair share of neurotics, authoritarians, and psychopaths, where whole organizations tend to reflect the neuroses of their constituent influential managers - whether paranoid, compulsive, depressive, or whatever (Cowton, 1998: 145).

Koistinen (1970: 2) argues that the effects of the Military-Industrial Complex on civil-military relations and military professionalism are profound and perverse. He contends that the business-military partnership destroys military professionalism. Proceeding from an elitist model of American society, he observes that a power elite made up of business, banking, and industrial leaders, dominate the government and controls the military. This elite, which relies "upon economic growth to solve most problems" has sought to maintain an American economic empire abroad in order to insure growth at home (Koistinen, 1970: 3).

Eisenhower stated, "No matter how much we spend for arms, there is no safety in arms alone. Our security is the total product of our economic, intellectual, moral, and military strengths (Koistinen, 1970: 13). As the push for globalization has caused profound changes for nation-states to accept the capitalistic system, many shifting priorities become apparent and essential for the MIC. Challenges against armament persist, as a desire for world peace to and to promote humanitarian and economic progress gains strength between times of war. Some proponents of moving from war time orientation to peace time endeavors have pushed to reduce the U.S. military budget by $40 to $100 billion per year by moving away from the Pentagon's outmoded "two war" strategy, canceling unnecessary cold war weaponry, and focusing U.S. policy on peacekeeping and conflict prevention, not arms sales and military buildups, as suggested by organizations such as Business Leaders for Sensible Priorities (Hartung, 1998).

Many leaders not wed to the MIC support regional and international efforts to cut military spending, such as the Year 2000 campaign to reduce military spending and the proposal for a moratorium on the export of advanced weaponry to Latin America, which have been spearheaded by Nobel Laureate Dr. Oscar Arias and organizations such as Demilitarization for Democracy, the Council on Economic Priorities, and the Carter Center (Hartung, 1998).

However, juxtaposed against peace initiatives is the reality that the U.S. government has characterized its current war campaign as a "two-front" war, further justifying existing military strategies for maintaining and even expanding its state of war preparedness while debunking the outcries of critics against the notion of a two-front war. It is highly unlikely that the MIC, with all of its invested manufacturing hardware and technologies, along with all the politicians and senior bureaucrats who drink from the same troths, will sit idly by, to allow pacifists to reduce its highly profitable enterprises. Historical facts point to a "smoking gun", that strongly suggests politicians, industrialists, and military brass all lie in the same bed, which they make appear to be in the national interests of the electorate. The irony is that the American electorate, whose will and interest is supposedly served in an ethical manner by its representatives, has given way to political and economic policies that reflect the architecture of the elite members who control the MIC. It's highly probable that "wars and rumors of war" shall persist for a time to come.

REFERENCES

Albrecht, D. (Ed.). (1995). *World War II and the American dream. How wartime building changed a nation.* Washington DC: The MIT Press.

Baack, B., and Ray, E. (1985). The political economy of the origins of the military-industrial complex in the United States. *Journal of Economic History*, Volume 45, Issue2, (June), 360-375. Retrieved October 7, 2001 from JSTOR database.

Baldwin, W. L. (1967). *The structure of the defense market 1955-1964.* Durham, N.C.: Duke University Press.

Baumgartner, J. S. (1970). *The lonely warriors. Case for the military-industrial complex.* Los Angeles, CA: Nash Publishing.

Benson, B. (1998). *To serve and protect: privatization and community in criminal justice.* New York, NY: New York University Press.

Clifford, J. G. (1990). Bureaucratic politics. *The Journal of American History*, Vol. 77, Issue 1 (June), 161-168. Retrieved October 7, 2001 from JSTOR database.

Coffman, E. M. (1984). The new American military history. *Military Affairs,* Vol. 48, Issue 1 (Jan.), 1-5. Retrieved October 7, 2001 from JSTOR database.

Cowton, C., and Crisp, R. (Ed.). (1998). *Business ethics. Perspectives on the practice of theory.* Oxford, UK: Oxford University Press.

Dumas, L. J. (Ed.). (1995). *The socio-economics of conversion from war to peace.* Armonk, NY: M.E. Sharpe.

Gansler, J. S. (1980). *The Defense Industry.* Cambridge, MA: The MIT Press.

Hartung, W. D. (1998). Defense authorization and appropriations bills, July 2, 1998. Comparisons of House and Senate F.Y. 1999: *Center for Strategic and Budgetary Assessments*. World Policy Institute. Retrieved November 13, 2001 from http://www.foreignpolicy-infocus.org/papers/micr/notes.html" \t "_parent

Huntington, S. P. (1982). American ideals versus American institutions. *Political Science Quarterly*, Vol. 97, Issue 1 (Spring), 1-37. Retrieved November 4, 2001 from JSTOR database.

Karpoff, J. M., Lee, D. S., and V. P. Vendrzyk. (1999). Defense procurement fraud, penalties, and contractor influence. *The Journal of Political Economy*, Vol. 107, Issue 4 (Aug.), 809-842. Retrieved November 4, 2001 from JSTOR database.

Koistinen, P. A. (1970). The "industrial-military complex" in historical perspective: The interwar years. *The Journal of American History*, Vol. 56, Issue 4 (Mar.), 819-839. Retrieved October 7, 2001 from JSTOR database.

Koistinen, P. A. C. (1980). *The military-industrial complex. A historical perspective.* New York, NY: Praeger Publishers.

Lotchin, R. W. (1970). The city and the sword: San Francisco and the rise of the metropolitan-military complex 1919-1941. *The Journal of American History*, Vol. 65, Issue 4 (Mar.), 996-1020. Retrieved November 4, 2001 from JSTOR database.

Mintz, A. (1992). *The political economy of military spending in the United States.* New York, NY: Routledge.

Molander, E. A. (1976). Historical antecedents of military-industrial criticism. *Military Affairs*, Vol. 40, Issue 2 (Apr.), 59-63. Retrieved November 4, 2001 from JSTOR database.

Moskos, C. C., Jr. (1976). The military. *Annual Review of Sociology*, Vol. 2 (1976), 55-77. Retrieved November 4, 2001 from JSTOR database.

Peterson, P. E. (1990). The rise and fall of special interest politics. *Political Science Quarterly*, Vol. 105, Issue 4 (Winter), 539-556. Retrieved November 4, 2001 from JSTOR database.

Pursell, C.W., Jr. (1972). *The military-industrial complex.* New York, NY: Harper & Row.

Reich, M. (1972). Does the U.S. economy require military spending? *The American Economic Review*, Vol. 62, Issue 1/2, 296-303. Retrieved October 7, 2001 from JSTOR database.

Risse-Kappen, T. (1991). Public opinion, domestic structure, and foreign policy in liberal democracies. *World Politics*, Vol. 43, Issue 4 (Jul., 479-512. Retrieved October 7, 2001 from JSTOR database.

Sandholtz, W., Michael Borrus, M., et al. (1992). *The highest stakes. The economic foundations of the next security system.* New York, NY: Oxford University Press.

Tyler, P. (1986). *Running critical. The silent war, Rickover, and General Dynamics.* New York, NY: Harper & Row.

Ullmann, J. E. (1985). *The prospects of American industrial recovery.* Westport, CN: Quorum Books.

The Impending New World Order will institutionalize racism and racial genocide.

In the period since the AMERICA entered WW2 in 1941, the world has witnessed human atrocities against humans on a level never before recorded in history, including dropping two nuclear bombs, concentration camps, and genocide. The violence that followed WW2 was in many ways equally abhorrent, if not more so. The civil rights struggles, the Vietnam War, assassinations of JFK, MLK, RFK, Malcolm, Gandhi, and many lesser known patriots and humanitarians set the stage for contemporary state and non-state acts of violence.

The horrific inhumanity of the Jewish Holocaust was only a few decades later followed by Pol Pot's Khmer Rouge slaughter of 2.4 million Cambodians. Idi Amin was known to laugh out loud when slaughtering hundreds of thousands of his own people in Uganda, the Tutus and Hutus killed each other in Rwanda between 500K to 1 million people, and China has witnessed the executions, imprisonment, starvation and torture of at least 50 million people during Mao's reign of horrors. It has not been a peaceful world, as technology has advanced the efficiency and effectiveness of violence, despite the so called Cold War nuclear deterrence.

Atrocities fostered or sponsored by Western political/military elites continued, who while espousing grand humanitarian ideals, have often betrayed the very principles they pretend to profess. Isn't the life of an African, or Asian, or Jew equally worth that of a Briton, American, German, or Swede? I surmise from standard of living statistics, that in the scales of the First World Hegemon, the answer is an emphatic "NO." Therein lies the basis of the international struggle between peoples, races, and ethnic groups. American history provides prime examples of First World tactics, as the genocide of Native Americans followed a pattern of false promises, broken treaties, and military violence, and African-Americans still suffer poverty, violence, and disease in alarmingly disproportionate levels, almost 140 years after slavery was abolished in the United States of America.

What does the First World Hegemon want that entails tolerance of inhumanity in non-white states, often supporting oppressive regimes in Third World nations, which it attempts to prevent in Europe? The historical colonialist mentality still runs strongly through the blood lines of Europe's elites; only the revisionist strategy for world domination no longer lies in direct military confrontation, but in global economic control and domination, juxtaposed by military intimidation. Their vision continues to be one of a united Europe as the center of civilization, a feat first attempted by European royalty, and now made possible by the creation of multi-national corporate conglomerates owned by European and American elites. What they weren't able to accomplish with real people, they now are achieving through fictional entities (legal immortal corporations) and the utilization of technology.

Europe is in fact no more than a fictional continent created to satisfy an egomaniacal self-aggrandizing overcompensating need to deny their early backward and warring heritage. Europe is not physically a continent, but merely the western end of the Asian continent. This drive to create fictional entities (corporations), fictional (and worthless) global debtor monetary systems, deceptive and untruthful marketing, political, and bureaucratic institutions and ideals are all part of their larger scheme of world domination. The First World Anglo-Germanic European-American plan for world domination is essentially the same in principle as it was when "The sun never set on the British Empire", only the methods have been disguised and repackaged to appear beneficial to the peace and economic progress of the developing world. It's a sales pitch that is leading the Third World eventually to genocide.

The smoke screen for the new world order is the accelerating dependency of developing world markets on the Western monetary system, the creation of a future justification for military intervention to protect Western assets, and the future wholesale rape of third world resources as repayment to World Bank members. The gradual genocide of Third World peoples through poverty, disease, racism, class warfare, violence, and military interventions (conventional, genetic, and nuclear) are methods of genocide. At the rate AIDS is decimating the population in Sub-Saharan Africa, NATO and UN troops, backed by First World corporate interests, will be called on in the future to "stabilize" Africa's infrastructure, as a pretext to develop its vast stores of natural resources for western products and consumption. The "silk road" to the eventual rape of Africa will be carved by bulldozers and the tracks of military vehicles. Many scholars support the primary hypothesis that the First World's intentions and actions result in the genocide of Third World people.

Few politicians or academicians will publicly admit or profess to discern the reality that stares down humanity today, and the likely outcomes of global political-economic policies dictated by the First World bloc of nations that comprises the white race. Their methods of self-propagation are many, including technological advantage, genetic weapons, economic destabilization, cultural imperialism, and first strike nuclear projection. Is it their goal to eventually limit world population to 2 billion humans, comprised of 1 billion whites (Alphas), and 1 billion colored races (Betas and Gammas, but no Deltas and Epsilons)? Is their hidden agenda to rid the world of the poor, illiterate, disabled, retarded, and non-elites over 60 that comprises over 80 percent of the planet's colored races, who will never to collect Social Security and Medicare benefits, thereby saving government trillions of dollars in America alone, not counting other nations.

Applying a global market economy paradigm, the Betas would serve the Alphas by producing goods and services from industries owned by the Alphas. According to Marxist theory, the Alphas would own the means of production, and the Betas would supply the labor. The Alphas (boursequoise) would obtain the best, with the lesser grade products available to the Betas (workers class). This "ideal" configuration will save the planetary environment by eliminating pollution from developing nations, massive waste products of human consumption, and the depletion of natural resources by an exploding world population (projected to reach 30 billion by 2100, if supportable by earth). The world would become

69

relatively stable because the white hegemony of so-called democratic states will be able to manage world resources according to the WTO & World Bank "standards." Developing nations, weakened by AIDS and diseases from GM (genetically modified) foods, will depend on the West to assist them, which will instead present a Trojan horse, the appearance of benign humanitarian aid, laced with genetic disease, political corruption, and economic dependency.

I.   The First World Hegemony's Anti-Third-World Genocide Strategy

A.   Economic dominance by the World Bank; dependency of developing nations' economies under the threat of monetary destabilization. The west is waiting for AIDS to decimate and weaken African and Asian governments to the point they may step in to "restore order and for humanitarian reasons", install corrupt puppet governments, and then export the natural resources of those continents while enslaving their peoples to supply cheap labor for products of western consumption.

B.   Cultural imperialism via the Internet, music, movies, clothing, food, and other deceptive marketing ploys to "sanitize" the world of non-western ideas, customs, cultures, and religions that do not conform to the ideal profit making motive of the global market system.

C.   Political colonialism via infectious spread of "scientific management" and other western legal and bureaucratic concepts, and through bribery and corruption of developing world governmental elites. Utilization of food and medicines as coercive strategies.

D.   Military domination by embargo of developing nuclear states, Supporting destabilization of non-cooperative states, projecting secret genetic and viral warfare materials into the Third World (e.g., AIDS, genetically modified foods), developing a nuclear missile shield, and targeting nukes at developing Third World nations as future nuclear extortion.

The ABM system and the projection of First World nuclear and economic power against the Third World are parts of a secretly formulated strategy to give world dominance and control to Euro-America. History and contemporary events indicate that there exist a real (secret), though subtle conspiracy among the Anglo-Germanic elites (and their white American descendants) who control world resources to maintain their superior position through policies that directly or indirectly result in the genocide of the world's non-whites.

References:

Christopher Keith Hall. "The First Five Sessions of the UN Preparatory Commission for the International Criminal Court (in Current Developments)." *American Journal of International Law*, Vol. 94, No. 4. (Oct., 2000), pp. 773-789.

Carole Nagengast. "Violence, Terror, and the Crisis of the State." *Annual Review of Anthropology*, Vol. 23. (1994), pp. 109-136.

Jonathan Benthall. "Fox Among the Lambs." *Anthropology Today*, Vol. 5, No. 3. (Jun., 1989), pp. 1-2.

Liisa H. Malkki. "Refugees and Exile: From "Refugee Studies" to the National Order of Things." *Annual Review of Anthropology*, Vol. 24. (1995), pp. 495-523.

Debora Shuger. "Irishmen, Aristocrats, and Other White Barbarians" *Renaissance Quarterly*, Vol. 50, No. 2. (Summer, 1997), pp. 494-525.

Kyle Grimes. "The Entropics of Discourse: Michael Harper's Debridement and the Myth of the Hero." *Black American Literature Forum*, Vol. 24, No. 3. (Autumn, 1990), pp. 417-440.

M. Estellie Smith. "The Process of Sociocultural Continuity." *Current Anthropology*, Vol. 23, No. 2. (Apr., 1982), pp. 127-142.

Chapter 3 – The new world order paradigm will institute inequities and racism

Racial inequities will become institutionalized in the new world economic and political order for several reasons, including:

- The entrenched power and economic elites will resist changing the global financial and global trade paradigm that has guaranteed them wealth
- Existing national economic inequities that already exist will persist
- National and regional economies are pieces of puzzles on the global board game of economic dominance and power brokering that maintains benefits

and the advantageous financial structure for the wealthy elites

- The general distribution of races into specific economic roles in specific niches in the global economic machine reflects existing global racial paradigm, of which the American racial landscape is a representational microcosm. For example, the poorest people are Africans, and in by comparison to whites and other races in America, blacks account for a disproportionately high representation of the poor. Asians are second only to whites in terms of financial success, both globally and in the U.S. The Hispanics are generally the lower middle class or poor both globally and in America, but on the whole do better than African-Americans and Africans. Other ethnic groups such as Jews and Arabs and other Middle East ethnic people are not considered a race per se, but more often than not are classified globally as part of the white race (but of course Aryans, Swedes, Germans and other white Europeans would differ on that classification and would prefer to categorize Jews and Arabs as Semitic peoples rather than as whites – Caucasians.

Is global racial genocide necessary and inevitable?

In the case of international relations, Waltz opined that state interactions, human relations, and functional differences within and between states has no real consequences, that the only factors of importance is the structural positioning of states as units that compete for survival through self-help self-propagation activities in competition with other states to determine who has the greatest degree of power (military-economic). It is the structure or positioning of power that stimulates the games states feel compelled to play to protect themselves against current and potential enemies, which determines consequences in the anarchic global disorder.

The issue of social contract per Thomas Hobbes, and how the state uses police force to intimidate its citizens to comply with its laws was discussed. Other intellectuals have written about social contract, such as Rousseau, who viewed *Social Contract* as a way to alleviate, among other things, the main cause of our evils. Rousseau felt that morals seem to be of two types: that which is moral in being "established" by "a sort of convention" as men begin to associate together,

72

and a "political" form that is moral in the sense of being "authorized" by the consent of man as a social contract. Rousseau felt that humans exist purely as physical beings, possessed solely of physical instincts, passions, and faculties; and man originally lacked moral needs or passions, or conscious regards for their fellow humans. Waltz views states as purely physical structures, possessed solely of the instinct of self-preservation corresponding to their power position in an anarchistic world, without regards to moral needs, passions, or conscious regards for humanity.

Few politicians or academicians publicly admit the reality that oppresses humanity today, the outcomes of global political-economic policies dictated by the First World bloc of nations that comprises the white race. Their methods of self-propagation are many: technology, control of capital, cultural imperialism, neo-colonialism, genetic/biological/viral/chemical weapons, and first strike nuclear projection. Is it their goal to eventually limit world population, primarily by reducing the number of Third World people who comprise 80 percent of the human race, and account for over 95% of the world's population growth?

The justification for "trimming back" world population is two fold: 1) conserving the planetary environment by reducing pollution from developing nations, and 2) reducing the depletion of natural resources by an exploding world population (projected to reach 30 billion by 2100, if supportable by earth). The world would become relatively stable because the white hegemony of so-called democratic states will be able to manage world resources according to the IMF and World Bank "standards." Developing nations, weakened by AIDS and diseases from GMO (genetically modified) foods, will depend on the West to assist them, which will instead present a Trojan horse, the appearance of benign humanitarian aid, laced with genetic disease, political corruption, and economic dependency; essentially the same strategy deployed against Native Americans by the U.S. Army through the spread of smallpox in blankets.

The First World Hegemony has historically implemented an anti-Third-World genocidal strategy that continues today through *economic disequilibria's* and other forms of socio-economic and political-cultural displacements. Population-to-resources, population-to-capital, racial, and cultural factors fail to explain the historical as well as the cross-national variation in economic development.

Economic dominance by the IMF and World Bank reinforces dependency of developing nations' economies under the threat of monetary destabilization caused by runaway debt. As AIDS decimates and weaken Africa, and increasing becomes a major public health concern in Asia and Latin America, government debt has reached the point where many Third World nation-states are essentially owned by creditor nations through the international monetary exchange system enforced by the IMF and World Bank. The First World installs corrupt puppet governments in the Third World, and rapes the natural resources of those continents while essentially enslaving their peoples to supply cheap labor for products of western consumption.

Abernethy noted in the first quarter of 1989, elite nationals of the Third World's 15 largest debtor nations were holding US $340 billion in foreign banks, up from less than $100 billion in 1980. The elites of Third World nations who support First World economic programs are allowed to pillage and plunder their own lands, as long as their actions serves the North. No doubt these numbers are paltry sums by today's standards where hidden wealth from corruption is unchecked.

In Nigeria, a stark illustration of World-Bank-designed, managed, and administered structural adjustment planning caused the currency (Naira) to devalue to $0.08 from a high of $1.80, and the creation of incentives for agrarian capital investment caused the monthly minimum wage to decline from $201 (1981) to $16 (1990). Consequently, the reliability of statistical evidence turned out by the World Bank to justify structural adjustment plans and sectored reform proposals is doubted, making the usefulness of such plans for African counties suspect. By 1988, 20 African governments accepted IMF stabilization programs and 22 had adopted World Bank adjustment policies. Austerity, currency devaluation, price reform, market discipline, and privatization ensued, resulting a massive transfer of governing power from formerly sovereign states to IMF/World Bank bureaucracies. The reality of decades of IMF/World Bank coercive economic management policies has been to drive down African living standards, and to disrupted their political, tribal, social, economic, cultural, and spiritual infrastructure.

Lubeck provides another clear example of this misbegotten IMF/World Bank strategy. In Nigeria, industries expanded rapidly during the 1970s, but later withered from lack of foreign exchange, as income once engorged by oil revenues that peaked at $25.3 billion in 1980, rapidly fell to $6.3 billion in 1986 under IMF/World Bank mandated structural adjustments. The UN's Economic Commission for Africa (ECA) insisted that the World Bank's deflationary policies destroyed Africa's productive basis for recovery, encouraged nonproductive speculation, undermined Africa's industrialization, and threatened the social fabric of African societies. The ECA strongly argued that Africa's problems were structural, arising from colonial-origin commodity system- problems that can not be resolved by short-term shock treatments.

To further exacerbate the economic problems of the Third World, western nations try to find substitutes for what it buys by advancing scientific and technological discoveries. Many less developed countries export a single crop or commodity to raise capital, in a time when capital is flowing from the poor to the rich countries ($93 billion for the years 1983-87 - World Bank), investment funds to less developed nations are very limited. Western scientific advancement stands to make Third World commodities superfluous to the North. On the other hand, First World nations dictate the retail price of oil, an essential to Third World economies. While the Institut Francais due Petrole predicts a 25 to 50 percent reduction in the cost of extracting oil, they estimate the price of crude oil will increase 65 percent. At the retail level, oil prices can rise while extraction costs fall because retail prices determined by supply (which can be manipulated) and demand (which rarely decreases). The Third World is held in a noose, which tightens as the western demand for natural resources and commodities from the South decrease due to scientific and technological advancements in the North, coupled with First World manipulated higher retail crude oil prices, that exacerbates the South's financial crisis.

Countries with high per capita incomes have comparably higher capital levels of production than those with low incomes. The countries of the Third World use relatively little capital, and those of the First World are capital rich, with most of the world's capital deposited into North America, western Europe and Japan. As the gap in per capita incomes between the rich and poor nations has increased over time, poor countries continue to fall further behind their potential.   The

Chinese Delegation to the U.N. argued that the condition of a nation is affected by its social system and the political and economic conditions existing domestically and internationally. They insist that it is mainly due to aggression, plunder and exploitation by the imperialists, particularly the superpowers that the Third World remains poor, adding that the widening gap between MDCs and LDCs is due to the old international economic order which increases inequalities, pursues external domination, foreign occupation, colonialism, racial discrimination, apartheid and neo-colonialism in all its forms, resulting in great obstacles to the full emancipation and progress of the developing countries.

LaRouche warns, as long as the IMF system, and its related strategies exist in their present form, regional states must avoid the ruinous effects that would result from such measures fostered by an already doomed IMF system. The needed reorganization of the international financial and monetary systems requires a structural reform in composition of categories of employment, investment, and credit-flows, to return to goals and standards which are consistent with the operating objectives of dependent governments.

The First World is based upon a *historical culture of violence*, and spreads its culture in modern times through neo-colonialism and cultural imperialism via modernization and reform programs forced or exported to the Third World as marketing ploys to "sanitize" the world of non-western ideas, customs, cultures, and religions that do not conform to the political ideology and capitalistic profit motive that drives the westernized global market system.

There exist ample historical evidence to confirm the First World is based on a culture of violence. Early Caucasian barbarians were a cruel and violent people, preoccupied with war, and were the racial founding stock for most of northern Europe. Roman historians wrote of the pervasive violence of northern European society, noting that the Germans spent all their lives in hunting and warlike pursuits because they had "no taste for peace" but consider "war and plunder" the only honorable pursuits. Among Europeans, strength determines status, and the warrior societies were ruthless and aristocratic; in Gaul only the Druids and warriors "are of any account or consideration", as the common people were typically treated almost as slaves. The Anglo-Irish were constantly occupied by endless petty warfare, even into present day times. Their culture was typified by strong kinship loyalties, lawlessness, and predatory violence which came to characterize the English aristocracy, who "consider that nothing brings you more honor than wholesale slaughter."

The upper classes felt "superior" to the lower, and members of the wealthy bourgeoisie assumed many of the attitudes of the aristocracy, including the self-adulating notion of genetic superiority. Blatant examples of cultural imperialism based upon the notion of white racial and cultural supremacy continues to be a subliminal driving force in First World domestic and international policies. During the 1920's the racial and ethnic diversity of the American population produced a mass interest in a racial eugenics movement. Increased concern over the low fertility of the white upper classes along with paranoia over the "race suicide" of superior Anglo-Saxons led to advocacy of "positive" eugenics (including increasing the fertility of the genetically superior) and "negative" eugenics (causing the "inferior stocks" to reduce their fertility). Hodgson observes that populations are still being shaped to conform to racial or ethnic preferences and genocide, a dramatic example of such shaping, is regularly attempted.

The repression of the real or imagined violence of dissidents is also justified, and enters through violent representations in popular culture, the media, television, films, the theater, and music. The forces of development and modernization combine to destroy traditional rural life in Third World countries, resulting in a constant pressure to emigrate from rural areas. Kasarda concludes that technology has fundamental influence on a society's social organization, and although societies create innovation and technology, it is the application of technology that is the cause of social change. These subordinated groups are the historical victims of western colonialism, or a result of the way colonial empires were carved up, and the resulting conflicts between nations, peoples, and minorities, often resulted in violent suppression, even genocide. Since 1945, state-sponsored violence toward ethnic and political groups caused more deaths, injuries, and human suffering than "all other forms of deadly conflict, including international wars and colonial and civil wars". Other costs are incalculable, including the extinction of languages, cultures, and ways of life, destruction of cultural and historical treasures, and loss or damage to residences, industry, and commerce. Nagengast questioned the kind of future that newly emerging elites desire in a world order, in which the possibilities for rejecting the power of the west is unlikely, where socialism has been discredited, and where there aren't other alternatives on the horizon. How, under this predicament, will new relationships of power and knowledge emerge and be resolved?

The Chinese stated before a UN committee, "In our opinion, the primary way of solving the... problem lies in combating the aggression and plunder of the imperialists, colonialists and neo-colonialists, breaking down the unequal international economic relations, winning and safeguarding national independence, and developing the national economy and culture independently and self-reliantly in the light of each country's specific conditions and differing circumstances, and raising the living standards of the people. It is highly doubtful that the North will agree with this Chinese perception.

Political colonialism through the spread of western legal and bureaucratic concepts, and through bribery and corruption of developing world governmental elites serves to bolster First World hegemonic power through Third World surrogates, puppets, and racketeers. The IMF/World Bank. Lubeck stated that IMF structural adjustment plans (SAPs) are externally planned, organized, and monitored, and they bypass, minimize, and privatize the former powers of the state. The crisis of the post-colonial state in Africa threatens to undermine the existing system of weakened states. The political changes are greatest in Nigeria, where between a quarter and a fifth of Africa's population lives. The alliance between the World Bank and reform-minded politicians is filled with corruption, mismanagement, waste, unrealistic crops, environmental degradation, and social tension. A new class of wealthy commercial farming strata with credit and political and commercial links to urban centers is becoming more powerful and prevalent, as peasants remain poor and powerless.

The Chinese perception of history is shared by a majority of Third World nations, and substantial numbers of Western historians, when they stated, "Social-imperialism asserts that 'only economic development with my aid can solve your population problem.' This is a ruse. It goes without saying that economic development is necessary for a country to emerge from poverty and solve its population problems. The point is that what social-imperialism calls 'economic development' is nothing but a fraud if it is not coupled with the fight against

78

imperialism and hegemonies and a change in the unequal international economic relations.'"

Nagengast reports the crisis of present day states results from its disparate concentration of power and the contradiction between it, and the demands of disempowered peoples who have created new positions that challenge the definitions of who and what ought to be repressed. The intelligentsias of the nineteen century and leaders of nationalist movements in Europe and North America had economic reasons for what they saw as a rational, democratic movements toward modernity and capitalism. The concepts of nation and nationalism in Europe and North America are the offspring of colonial expansion, religious wars, rationalism, and capitalism that serve as justification and political legitimization for certain notions of territorial, political, and cultural unity enforced by the hegemony of liberal thought and organization. Consequently, Nagengast observed "the world is in transition from strict acceptance of sovereign jurisdiction and non-intervention to more and more readiness to undertake... action, up to and including military action, that would in the past have been considered intervention in domestic affairs." Kasarda observed, "While it is true that social (e.g. religious/ethnic) and economic elites wield great power, their abilities to gain hegemony over a nation's future depend on capturing and holding the political machinery. These theorists post that coalitions organized around shared self-interest combine either to exert pressure on the state or to dominate it, and the express purpose of these activities is to generate laws that divert social surplus to special interests. Olson suggests that since natural resource endowments, differences in capital stocks, cultural variation in responses to economic incentives, the features of the international system are not sufficient to explain economic development. Consequently, it would seem the institutions and policies of countries would have to be important, as the politics of the First World pervasively intrudes into the governance of the Third World.

The First World uses calculated *military intimidation*, and support destabilizing non-cooperative states in the Third World and utilizes measured force to maintain economic and political hegemony. In addition to cultural propensities for violence, the First World developed philosophical justification for the need and desirability for violence and military actions. Malkki observed that wars have created tens of millions of displaced individuals and families originating in the Third World. The causes of their plight are conflicts kept alive mostly by superpower politics and by weapons manufactured in the rich countries, who export death and destruction to the Third World in exchange for importing the natural and partly processed products of the poor countries.

According Pasqualucci, a sustaining justification of western thought is that depopulation through war appears to be a natural phenomenon, as if nature itself wishes to prevent the human pretension to eliminate war forever. Thomas Hobbes felt it perfectly legitimate to establish colonies to solve the problems raised by overpopulation, adding, "in any case, a war of conquest appears here to be perfectly legitimate... when the excess of population in his own country becomes unbearable, the Sovereign 'has to', has the duty to, 'transplant,' if he can, the excess of population in another country, whether inhabited or not, and without being obliged to ask permission from anybody.

The North fear the warnings of the prophetic philosophers, intellectuals, and speculators of their time, such as Thomas Maltus and Thomas Hobbes, who would likely support paranoid doomsday scenarios, as justification for Northern warmongering. Hobbes believed Malhusian vision, when he stated that, "The development of mankind will come to an end "when all the world is overcharged with inhabitants"... therefore the only remedy for such a state of things is once again... a war of extermination... there will be no prisoners... because the scope of such a war is precisely that of making the space of the world as void as possible of inhabitants, to the point that the most frightful war of extermination will take place one day as the "last remedy of all." In his opinion, there is no doubt that the progress of mankind will end in a universal, apocalyptic conflagration, adding, "Behind the growth of the multitude in the Third World, there seems to be a messianic impulse, a thrust, to conquer the rest of the world in order to 'regenerate' it in the name of an ideology and a religion....in that 'perpetual and restless desire of power after power, that ceaseth only in death,....'" It's only too obvious that western political thinkers believe that the most efficacious way to save the world for the North is to make space, by eliminating the burgeoning populations of the South.

The prevailing First World view is that *overpopulation and ecological* pressures provide justification to consider and pursue surreptitious genocidal programs in the Third World. Malthus proposed a theory of overpopulation in a zero-sum game of survival, where unchecked overpopulation will eventually exhaust the world food supply. Based on Maltusian ideas, the First World has formulated the "overpopulation paradigm" that blames rapid population growth on poverty, illiteracy, and cultural propensies, typical of the Third World.

The Overpopulation Paradigm:

The UN's 1993 estimated population projected in 2020 is between 7.6 to 8.5 billion, however barely 20 years later, the world's population already stands at 7.1 billion, up from 5.5 billion people. Cohen observed that around 10,000 year ago, there were roughly 6 million people on Earth. Today, there are more than 7 billion people. The human population increased by a factor of about 1,000 in 10,000 years. Cohen made a similar projection applying the estimated 1995 population growth rate of 1.6 percent per year. If growth of 1.6 percent per year persists for 436 years, the population will have increased to at least 1,000 fold. If people and the planet can not absorb a tenfold, rather than a 1,000 fold increase in population size to 60 billion, then the present global growth rate cannot continue even another 150 years. The world's population has doubled over the post-war period, from 2.5 billion in 1950 to more than 5 billion in 1990, and is likely to more than triple between 1950 and the projected total of nearly 8 billion in 2020. Tapinos reported according to the UN, in 1970, the geographic distribution of human population in the world was 30 percent in developed areas, and 70 percent in less developed areas. In 1980, the ratio changed to 24 and 76 percent. In 1990, the population distribution exceeded 80 percent in less developed nations.

The First World refuses to recognize that the solution to overpopulation is to uplift the conditions of the Third World, who they blame for causing the degradation of the planet's resources, though in fact, it is the First World that consumes over 80% of the world's resources and contributes a similar percentage to its pollution, global warming, and species extinctions. The United States uses over half of all the raw materials consumed each year; as less than 1/15 (1970) of the world's population required more than the remaining part to maintain its overconsumptive position. As present trends continued, in 20 years, we will get much less than 1/15 of the population, and yet we may use some 80% of the resources consumed.   In 2000, the U.S. population was estimated to exceed 275 million people, compared to the world's 6.1 billion inhabitants, which accounts to approximately 4.5% of the world's population utilizing most of its nonrenewable resources.

Kremer notes demographic evidence clearly indicate that if population grows at finite speed when income is above a steady state, per capita income will rise over time. If population growth declines at high levels of income, per capita income will rise over time. However, data also suggest that higher levels of income and technology may reduce fertility by increasing wages and thus the value of time, by increasing education and the relative value of women's time. He concluded that population growth increases at low levels of income, then decreases in high levels of income.

Reacting to capitalist background and the Malthusian basis of Anglo-Saxon thinking, which viewed overpopulation as the cause of poverty, almost all developing countries favored the Marxist idea that the real cause of poverty was unequal distribution of wealth, both among and between countries, and that overpopulation was a symptom rather than a cause of the basic problem. The Third World argues that economic and social development, especially more equitable distribution of economic gains among the poorest areas, would be at least, if not more effective in reducing fertility as family-planning programs. Keyfitz explained that the less developed countries contain four-fifths of the world population, are responsible for nine-tenths of present population growth, and can expect 100 percent of the world's population growth during the first century of the new millennium. Consequently, they do not have the space, land, or the capital to support their exploding citizenry. The demand for their raw materials constituted the economic foundation on which they attempted their upward course, but scientific advances in developed nations has invented substitutes that undercut the need for Third World resources.

Wilmoth noted that the "orthodox" view of the disadvantages of rapid population growth and of the possibility for positive strategies to lower birthrates in less developed countries (LCDs) dominated political discussions of the topic during the 1960s and 1970s.   The dominant theme of the articles of this era was that population growth is rapid and threatens the welfare of human beings and other species. It was thought that rapid population growth threatened the very survival of the human species, due to finite limits on the availability of resources as land, water, and fossil fuels. They concluded that population growth must somehow be brought under control, either through limitations on reproduction or through an increase in the death rate. Since growth is limited by finite resources, the only sensible solution is to limit population size to a sustainable level. The North feared that inaction will eventually lead to ecological disasters that will result in widespread famine, disease, misery, and, potentially, the extinction of the human species. Yates predicted that overpopulation and underproduction in major nations of the Third World will result in great famines and pose future questions of life and death significance to the world community.

Wilmoth believes that growth produces population pressure that accentuates the threat to the stability of world political systems. Population pressure may lead nations to press outward from their borders in search of living space, or it may foster internal political instability, leading in some cases to revolutions. Population pressure has been the cause of past wars and will continue to be a source of future conflict if population growth is not controlled, adding, "Rapid population growth is disadvantageous, as overcrowding has negative effects on the quality of human existence... producing a general deterioration in the quality of the natural and social environments of human societies. Overcrowding brings in its train a host of adverse side effects, including urban congestion, pollution, shortages of housing and recreational space, and various forms of 'social pathology' that increases the role of governments at the expense of individual liberties."

This fear of potential extinction, drives the North to the argument based on a perception that one population (or sub-population) is losing or will lose control over some vital aspect of social and political life due to its relative decrease in numbers in comparison to other groups, and consequently, a race suicide framework materializes when population growth is viewed as unfavorably to the population fearful of losing control.   Without a globally coordinated concentrated effort to stabilize population size at a level far lower than currently projected, the earth's ecosystems and the living standards of increasing numbers of the world's

83

people will deteriorate. An immediate decrease in world population growth will provide time to make necessary changes, and to develop new technologies and alternative energy sources.

Brundtland reports that ninety percent of the world's population increase is occurring in developing countries, many of which are unable to feed their present population.   He suggests that the industrialized nations must change their production and consumption patterns to use less natural resources and cause less pollution, adding that development in poor countries must be planned to eliminate poverty, meet basic human needs, and to protect the environment. He notes that population growth must be slowed to allow sustainable development because poverty, overpopulation, and underdevelopment are all interlinked. The fastest population growth is burdening the poorest nations, which are least able to meet the needs of new births and to invest in their future. Brundtland concludes that the increasing numbers of people in poor countries are deteriorating the earth and creating permanent damage to the environment because they struggle to survive, and cannot be concerned with planning for a tomorrow that may never come. As a result, impoverished environments in turn lead to even greater poverty, and a vicious cycle is created.

Brundtland observes that any nation's main asset should be its population, lamenting, "But when that population grows too fast, it becomes a liability instead." He noted that a rapidly growing population stifles the best efforts to provide proper education, nutrition, health care and shelter, while the earning capacity of the labor force suffers, and problems are compounded as job opportunities don't keep pace with the numbers seeking jobs. As wages go down and poverty is exacerbated. He proposed enhancing the role of women to increased economic growth, reduced poverty, provide better child and family welfare, and to lower birth rates. He warns that if men avoid responsibility for their sexual habits, fertility, and health, and if they reject their parental obligations, it will be impossible to deal with population growth, and with sexually transmitted diseases, including AIDS.

Finkle observes that as more governments identify their "population problem" as rapid population growth, leaders of developing countries realize that the health of their societies is dependent on the ability to provide jobs, schools, housing, and health care for their citizens, all of which are made more difficult by rapid population growth. He proposes the need for reducing the rate of population growth in order to remove major obstacles to economic development.

Just how the North proposes to limit, reduce, and reverse population growth in the South is unclear. One thing is certain, the economic policies that western nations have implemented in regards to almost all of the Third World, have served to reduce economic development, which has resulted in faster population growth, and the institutionalizing of a vicious cycle of poverty, starvation, disease, and illiteracy. And among the elite power circles in the First World, there continues to be serious leanings by intellectuals and political thinkers to blame the Third World's burgeoning population for the evils of the world, for planetary deterioration, and environmental pollution that, if not arrested and reversed, will eventually threaten the very existence of the human species. Some "experts" may even feel that Third World genocide is a benevolent policy.

The Environmental Impact Paradigm:

Keyfitz believes that such things don't determine the real limit to global population growth as the availability of food, natural disasters, or wars, but instead in the number of people that can be supported by the biosphere without disrupting its sensitive balance. Mankind is but one species among many, each with a place in nature, and each threatened with destruction if it grows to the point where it destroys the very environment upon which its existence depends. He observes that humans must co-exist with the AIDS virus and Ebola in the same manner as man-induced imbalance, measles, malaria, and other diseases, warning that human activities must not interfere with the inanimate aspects of the Earth that are essential for his existence, such as the ozone layer that provides protection from carcinogenic rays from space. He questions whether humans have the will to make sacrifices now, to protect the planet for future generations against the terrible consequences that may result from excessive human population, which he terms "an unstoppable collapse that follows from irreversible changes of which there are plentiful examples in the past."

Environmentalists see the planet's condition today at risk in the face of the far reaching, and unprecedented changes that the human population and its activities are now causing. Global warming is one such major concern, for example, as average air temperature in Denmark has increased 1.75 degrees Centigrade in 125 years from 1875 to 2000. If this rate of global warming continues, the ice caps will gradually melt, causing the flooding of coastal towns and cities, and in some cases reducing entire nation-states into nonexistence. By the year 2100, as compared to 1990 levels, greater demand will cause dramatic increases in the production of energy from all sources, including; a 50 percent increase in fossil fuel, a doubling of biomass, a quadrupling of hydroelectricity, a nine-fold jump in nuclear energy, and a twelve-fold expansion in renewable energy technologies. This will cause atmospheric CO2 concentration in 2100 to increase from 355 ppm to a likely 500 ppm, a 40 percent increase from 1990 levels.

Grant provides additional global warming data, as an assessment confirmed a rise of between 0.3 deg. C to 0.6 deg. C in global mean surface temperature in the past century, and a related rise in global sea level of 10 to 25 cm. These rates will result in a temperature increase of of 1.0 deg. to 3.5 deg. C by 2100, which is far faster than any warming trend in the Earth's past 10,000 years. Global warming will cause a rise of 15 –95 cm in average sea level by 2100, and the changes in both temperature and sea levels will continue in the centuries beyond 2100 *even if greenhouse gas concentrations are stabilized at current levels*. He further predicts that a complete melting of the Antarctic and Greenland ice caps would raise sea levels about 70 to 100 meters. Grant concludes that to avoid the greenhouse effect scenario that is primarily caused by human activities, a human population of perhaps 2 or 3 billion could be sustained at a decent level, commenting that this suggestion is less radical than it sounds, as it is where we were two generations ago (circa 1950).

On the other hand, Cohen pointes to a theoretical projection of global population to the year 2150 (similar to that prepared by the United Nations, 1992) that assumes regional levels of fertility are constant at 1950 levels, while life expectancy increases; the calculated population of 694 billion in 2150 could not be fed with conventional agriculture and water sources because annual global rainfall would be insufficient to grow the crops required for food. The renewable freshwater supply of the Earth is too limited for sustained agricultural irrigation and fertility, even if every drop of the 110,000 cubic kilometers of annual rain falling on land were used domestically for agriculture, and if people ate only 2,350 calories per day, the estimates of the maximum theoretical population that could be supported on Earth would range from 82 billion to 369 billion.

Keyfitz brings forth an ethical dilemma by questioning what share of the remainder of our planet's capacity to absorb emissions is the First World entitled to, as compared to the claims of the Third World. How legitimate is the South's position if they fail to reduce population growth? While the North has for decades restrained its population to less than two children per couple, can the South realistically expect the same material standard of living when their families are producing three, four or more children per couple? How will the First World arbitrate the its claims the need to preserve resources for future generations against those of the present, while competing with the Third World for as much of the world's resources as the North needs.

Abernethy adds that waste and deterioration of natural resources is likely a normal practice because private and local incentives to conserve is insufficient due to demand and disbelief in scarcity, as consumers believe they are better off without a commitment to share. It's often assumed that the great disparities in world living standards are due primarily to overpopulation in poor countries. Olson explains that given technology, fixed amounts of land and other natural resources, and level stocks of capital goods, increasing labor at some point yields diminishing productivity and also result in diminishing returns to nature's ability to absorb wastes.

In summary, the conventional wisdom of the First World that links population growth to potentially irreversible economic degradation is founded on four postulates:

1) The Earth's renewable resources, such as fresh water and aridable land mass for food production, are limited as in a zero-sum end game.

2) Population growth, particularly in the Third World, if unchecked, or even reversed, will lead to catastrophic and irreversible damage to our planet's ecosystem.

3) The First World's interest in self-propagation at a high standard of living is best served by limiting population growth in the Third World,

preferably through strategies that limit or reverse their industrialization and population growth.

4) When increased human activities due to overpopulation impact the planet's closed biosphere to a point of diminished returns, great famines and disease will decimate the global population, primarily concentrated in the Third World.

In fact, each of these First World assumptions shifting blame primarily to Third World population growth in not only self serving, but erroneous in its very premises, which will be discussed later in this summary.

The First World has historically, routinely, and systematically implements policies that result in the degradation, reduction, and genocide against dark-skinned peoples, in particular the black race. The North characterizes itself by eloquent statements in support of human rights, but a closer examination of western history discloses a sinister methodology of speaking "in the name of" some apparent humanitarian principle, only later to act "in spite of" the very principles they espouse. In the name of Christian brotherhood, the wars fought during the (un)Holy Crusades killed hundreds of thousands of "pagans", in order to save their souls, no doubt. In the name of "freedom" from supposed communist tyranny, the North killed millions of innocent women, men, and children as non-combatant "collateral" damage in South East Asia. Even Northern terminology is euphemistically and eloquently stated to reduce the appearance of its inhumane actions, by reducing the faces of those slaughtered into nomenclature only applicable to property, such as "collateral damage", as in damaged freight.

Nagengast defines political violence as overt state-sponsored or tolerated violence, which   may or may not be direct violence. The violence between Hutus and Tutsi in Rwanda and Burundi; between Tamils and Sinhalese in Sri Lanka; between Latinos and indigenous peoples in Guatemala; and among Croats, Serbs, and Muslims in the Balkans, is tolerated or encouraged by states to create, justify, excuse, explain, or enforce disparate hierarchies and inequalities. These are incidents of state violence; and even though states may not appear on the surface to be primary agents, the deliberate acts of agents of the state cause mass starvation and similar economic or political misdeeds that result in widespread deaths, and even genocide.   Lubeck described the scale of crisis in Africa gives it no option but to rely on a "reformed state" to regulate activity; consequently, chaos, starvation, and disintegration of states through neocolonial structures will follow as neo-liberal policies are strictly enforced. He adds that without debt relief and concessionary grants, Africa's primary commodity exporters can never hope to pay off their external debts (i.e. 350% of GDP), no matter how many neoliberal reforms are instituted internally.

Even in the most developed nation in the world, Peterson notes that a poverty paradox is one manifestation of a general deterioration in American society and culture where the spreading of an underclass culture (primarily blacks) is "undermining" the country's productive capacity, family life, social integration, and, ultimately its political stability. Petersen remarks, "Those underclass groups, American blacks being the extreme case, were compelled to come to or were forcefully incorporated into the United States and, once there, were subjected to poverty, discrimination, and slavery, constructed for themselves a conflictual understanding of the country's social and political institutions as the product of class dominance, racial prejudice and discrimination, cultural exclusiveness, over which they had little control." Grimes stated that draft regulations of the 60s and 70s ensured that most of those sent Vietnam were the poor and the Blacks. One desire of white supremacists has always been the fantasy of an all white country, resulting in genocide, Indian massacres, slavery, manifest destiny, Detroit, East St. Louis, Watts, the Domestic War.

Chinta Strausberg, writing in The "Chicago Defender", the oldest Black daily newspaper in America, warns Blacks must never forget the African Holocaust where more than 50 million lives were destroyed due to western greed for material wealth, further quoting Dr. James Small, a New York professor, who said:

"...these acts were crimes against humanity. All these people died because someone was greedy and wasn't willing to work for it for themselves, so they forced other human beings to do it.... "And in the process, they took the lives of nearly 50 million men, women and children when we count those captured... killed on the ground in Africa, died in the dungeons waiting for slave ships from diseases and hunger, died in the middle passage coming to America in the time it took to get here in those slave ships and those that died on the plantations....Our life expectancy during the early part

89

of slavery was not much more than five years, and they didn't mind working us to death because it was easy to replenish us. "In that 500-year period, we lost almost 50 million people and there are those who want us to forget it like it never happened.... Every effort was made by the enslavers to take away and to deny the humanity of the African. They were treated as objects, less than human. The Europeans used us as if we were their property. When we talk about killing the African spirit, it refers to the intent of white supremacy the dehumanization of African people by enslavement. Hall reported that attached to the crime against humanity of enslavement was deprivation of liberty, forced labor, reduction of people into servitude, and trafficking in persons, particular women and children. Yates observed that humans destroy most species by destroying their habitats, rather than simply by killing them. Habitat destruction is a phenomenon rapidly occurring in the Third World, especially in Africa. Commenting on the plight of Africa, the Chinese U.N. Delegation stated "... colonialists and imperialists subjected... Africa... to brutal aggression and enslavement... and have not only plundered enormous social wealth from... Africa, but also engaged in human trafficking and evicted or slaughtered local inhabitants. Africa alone has lost as many as 100 million people in this way... the social productive forces in... African... countries were seriously sapped. The North has a long history of exploiting, enslaving, impoverishing and killing Blacks.

The United States of America hegemony, while marketing itself to the world as the defender of human rights, actually provides a platform that initiates, supports, and implements global genocide through surrogates and Third World agents. LaRouche reports a public declaration in the September 1946 edition of "The Bulletin of the Atomic Scientists", made by Bertran Russell, "who was emphatic in stating that he was promoting nuclear weapons for no other purpose but establishing world government. Russell insisted, then, and later, that the AMERICA and Britain should prepare to bomb the Soviet Union with nuclear weapons, for the contingency that Soviet General Secretary Josef Stalin might refuse to submit to transforming the United Nations Organization into an actual world government, thus eliminating the sovereignties of all of the world's nation-states."

90

Grimes observes that in Vietnam, the myth of America as liberator was in danger of collapse because during the Vietnam War, it was evident that American military forces was not liberating anyone, but was slashing blindly through the Vietnamese landscape murdering anyone, regardless of political persuasion. Singer argues that the largeness of current populations is not needed for progressive development or the maintenance of diversity, adding that if blunders result in a nuclear war, and thereby eliminate nine-tenths of the human lives on our planet, the scattered survivors would find themselves with the "appropriate" phenotype to enable a "wiser fresh start."

The U.S., long a supporter of war crimes trials for crimes against humanity, such as genocide, instead attempts to exempt itself from the legal jurisdiction of international courts to avoid the surrender of Americans. The chances that the United States will be able to win the exemption of Americans from the court's jurisdiction are diminishing rapidly. Consequently, political choices in the Third World often appear to be determined by taking positions contrary to those of the United States, based on a simplistic syllogism:

1. The United States advises a particular policy.

2. Any advice of the United States corresponds to its own interests and might be, or is likely contrary to our own national interests.

3. Conclusion: We should reject American policies.

This discussion of the structural components of violence and power as facets of First World hegemony, and its projection through racially based economic, cultural, and political imperialism, colonialism, and neocolonialism into the Third World. Utilizing various pseudo-intellectual justifications such as "racial superiority", "overpopulation", and "environmental deterioration", the North has implemented military and economic strategies to subjugate, exploit, and degrade the states and people of the South. The increasing alarm over an expanding world population, predominantly in the Third World, is in large part motivated by a western paranoia of both becoming overrun by non-white people, and a potential threat to human existence due to the possible exhaustion of natural resources required for survival. This notion of "race suicide" compels the North to consider and devise self-propagation scenarios and strategies that act to the detriment of developing and underdeveloped states, up to and including genocide.

As a result of First World fears, avarice, and immorality, Pope John Paul II noted that broad segments of public opinion justify certain crimes against life in the name of individual freedoms and rights. The emergence of a "veritable culture of death" is fostered by powerful cultural, economic and political forces, which encourage society to be overly concerned with efficiency. Consequently, from this point of view, the world has become in a certain sense, a war of the powerful against the weak. The Pope adds, "On a more general level, there exists in contemporary culture a certain Promethean attitude which leads people to think that they can control life and death by taking the decisions about them into their own hands. We see a tragic expression of all this in the spread of euthanasia, disguised and surreptitious or practiced openly and even legally... is sometimes justified by the utilitarian motive of avoiding costs which bring no return and which weight heavily on society. Thus it is proposed to eliminate malformed babies, the severely handicapped, the disabled, the elderly, especially when they are not self-sufficient, and the terminally ill. Nor can we remain silent in the face of other more furtive, but no less serious and real forms of euthanasia... Today not a few of the powerful of the earth are haunted by the current demographic growth and fear that the most prolific and poorest peoples represent a threat for the well-being and peace of their own countries.

The proposed American "National Missile Defense" (NMD) system will permit the unchallenged projection of First World nuclear and economic power against the Third World. History has shown that the North routinely practices policies that ensure Euro-American global military, political, and economic dominance and control over world resources, to maintain their superior position utilizing policies that directly or indirectly result in the genocide of the world's non-white people, and destruction of Third World cultures, states, and regional economies.

How can Third World nations use the international forum to discredit the First World's recurring attempts to legitimize and justify genocidal policies as the ultimate solution to Third World overpopulation that purportedly threatens the quality and existence of human life on Earth? There are intermediary steps that must be taken to forestall the North's use of weapons of mass destruction as a population control measure. First, the international community must agree to arrest population at current levels through sensible reproductive quotas and policies, and to reduce overall native populations over time. Couples must be limited to no more than two offspring, as a realistic population stabilization policy. This quota should result in an eventual drop in overall population due to an excessive rate of mortality from environmental causes and infant mortality over live births. In recent decades, China has made significant advances in developing their economy while successfully controlling population growth. The natural population growth rate dropped to 1.154 percent in 1983, from 2.089 percent in 1973, and the people's living standards have improved. The Chinese family planning and population controlled-growth policies, in tandem with planned economic development has been the correct model for China, and may be an effective model for the rest of the Third World.

Following China's one-child example, the UN should encourage a global two live births per couple policy as a means to stabilize population, encourage a redistribution of excess First World resources to improve living standards and GDP, especially in less developed countries. Increasing the development and modernization of LDCs enhances global political and social stability that is a requisite for capital growth, which reinforces a cycle of increased modernization and development. Greater regional, common market, and global commons trade should "raise the tide for all ships, large and small". It is likely the paradigm of uneven distribution of global resources from poor nations to the rich will continue, but First World nations know only too well that increasing economic development of LDCs will likely result in decreasing world population through peaceful, rather than traditional violent means. Grant (205) weighs in on population policy, insisting parents need have no more than two children to carry on their family, and while it was once necessary to have many children so that some might survive to maturity, that is no longer true in most parts of the world.

While every living being has a natural urge and right to reproduce, even in nature, excessive numbers of any species eventually lead to catastrophic suffering and mortality. In order to avert a mass mortality scenario for human beings, sensible international agreements and political policies must be made. China's one birth per couple policy is a sensible effort to decrease that nations population through non-violent means. Depending upon overall population demographics, international benchmarks might become necessary, such that nations with populations over 300 million must actualize a 1.5 live births per couple quota (as expressed by 3 live births per every two couples, utilizing a lottery system). Similarly, nations with 500 million or more populations must agree to a 1.25 births per couple quota. Nations with 1 billion or more population must agree to 1 birth per couple quota, or institute a national lottery, followed by fertility sterilization.

Only through implementing proactive non-violent population control strategies, coupled with improving non-polluting technologies, and providing capital incentives for political and social stabilization, will the First World lose its temptation to make genocidal "first strikes" against the developing world. History has shown that the First World hegemony will not do anything that is against its self-interests. Consequently, LDCs must take steps to negotiate strategies that will encourage First World capital investment in exchange for population control, returning a reasonable "Return On Investment" to the First World.

The North owns and exploits over 80 percent of the world's non-renewable resources, consequently, it must restrain its avarice, and recognize its responsibility to redistribute at least a small percentage of excessive wealth, and restrict its consumption of world resources to no more than current levels. The First World must act morally and responsibly to restrain its temptation to project violence. The First World must practice what it preaches; act as the champion of human rights which its philosophical and legal tenets profess. If the First World assists the development of LCDs in exchange for non-violent population control measures, the tide will rise for all humanity as biosphere destruction is arrested. But how likely are the First World elites and LCDs likely to adopt such rational approaches to the zero-sum game of population control and environmental protection? History and current environmental scans suggests a mixed and uncertain future.

Blands (25-26) stated that it required 35 years from1965 for 3.3 B people to doubled in 2000 to 6.5 B people, a population that is inadequately fed by the cultivation of 56 percent of the world's arable land. If agricultural productivity in the less developed countries could be raised to that in the United States, there would be an enormous increase in agricultural output. By increasing the existing levels of agricultural production, as well as the potential for increasing the amount of land under cultivation, he found that the "potential gross cropped area would then be sufficient for 38-48 billion people, or 10-13 times the present human population of the earth. If these projections are reasonably accurate, it appears the world can still accommodate limited human population growth beyond the current 6.2 B people to 38 B, limited by arable land, or 82 B from natural rainfall limits.

Clinton warns that a population strategy targeting Third World birth rates could be taken as a form of repression, as a preventive form of class and racial genocide, and if all of population policy focused on limiting births, based on perceived upper limits of supportable birth rates, this would equate to a genocidal act of the rich against the poor, the white against the colored races, and the West against the East. Boot opines, "The global social structure is based on selfishness, maintained by power-play, marred by short-run vision, and managed by crisis-hopping. The rich, while luxuriating in wealth, pay lip-service to serious problems shared by all, but lack inclination to act decisively. In the back of their minds they surely believe in the survival of the fittest. They are the fittest. The poor, distrustful of the rich, are so burdened with short-run survival that the long-run problems seem insignificant."

Finnin discloses that "it requires about one-third of the world's annual extraction of nonrenewable resources to support the 6 percent of the world's population in the United States at the per capita level to which it is thought the rest of the world should become accustomed." He estimates that if U.S. levels of technology could prevail worldwide, current resources could support no more than18 percent of the world's population at U.S. levels, with nothing left over for the remainder 82 percent. Paradoxically, without the labor services of the lower 82 percent, the rich 18 percent would not be as rich as they might think.

Keohane summarizes the international predicament by stating, "The sources of hegemony therefore include sufficient military power to deter or rebuff attempts to capture and close off important areas of the world political economy. But in the contemporary world, at any rate, it is difficult for a hegemon to use military power directly to attain its economic policy objectives with its military partners and allies." He adds, "Hegemony require deference to enable them to construct a structure of world capitalist order. It is too expensive, and perhaps self-defeating, to achieve this by force; after all, the key distinction between hegemony and imperialism is that a hegemony, unlike an empire, does not dominate societies through a cumbersome political superstructure, but rather supervises the relationships between politically independent societies through a combination of hierarchies of control and the operation of markets. Hegemony rests on the subjective awareness by elites in secondary states that they are benefiting...."

In conclusion, a united international community can make inroads to resist and eventually change First World hegemonic paranoia by debunking the legitimacy of long held pseudo-scientific theories on the causes of poverty, population growth, ecological degradation, and economic-political competition in the perceived zero-sum end game from consumption of world resources.

1) The Earth's resources are relatively untapped. Our deepest wells barely scratch the Earth's crust, and cheaper technology can be developed to increase global storage and supplies of fresh water (desalinization, etc.), as biotechnology continues to improve crop yields and the arability of land. Technology can also be called upon to restore the arability of topsoil in non-productive regions, and topsoil erosion can be ameliorated by digging into the crust to access the rich minerals contained in the Earth's mantle, as in volcanic magma. The rich resources of Africa and many areas of the world are essentially untapped, but these areas must not be exploited to the detriment of its native populations, who should instead be the beneficiaries of development.

By removing the erroneous presumption that resource consumption is non-renewable and non-recyclable, the world can reject the notion of limits in a zero-sum end game, and begin to search for new sources of abundance located deeper in the crust, in volcanoes, geysers, and in the Earth's deep oceans and mantle. Alternative energy sources, based on discoveries in new quantum physics that can generate electricity and motion by harnessing strong gravitational forces, near frictionless materials, and electro-magnetic applications could be developed once "big oil interests" are politically reduced, as new technologies replace the need for burning fossil fuels for energy.

2) Population growth, particularly in the Third World, would likely follow First World patterns of natural reduction that follows economic development, and

the liberation of women from their roles as birthing machines. In the male dominated and chauvinistic world, men must take greater procreative responsibility, utilizing birth control methods to prevent childbirths when they are unable to afford the expense of childrearing. Having children simple to satisfy the egocentric desire to continue one's lineage is insufficient rationale for expecting women to give birth. Each child born into the world has a right, and deserves to have at a minimum, food, shelter, education, and love, with the goal of liberty and self-actualization. Again, technological breakthroughs stand to assist family planning efforts, through reversible sterilization, surrogate birthing utilizing xeno-placental techniques, and other strategies that emphasize responsible parenting choices. Overbeek (191) explores the possibility of adding contraceptive agents to certain foods, providing another drug to neutralize the sterilizing effects of the contraceptive agent for those who desire pregnancy. If it were added to certain foods only, then only those wanting to be sterile could consume those foods.

The First World's self-propagation at a high standard of living can best be assured by global partnership, and not wanton exploitation of the Third World. The waste that exist in the North alone, is more than sufficient to maintain the developing world, consequently, conservation in the First World allows the South to improve its economies, and through non-pollution strategies, both West and the East can become responsible partners to, and not abusers of our planet. The traditional "competition" paradigm must necessarily be replaced by a "partnership" paradigm.

4)   Human activities due to population growth need not have a negative impact on the planet's closed biosphere. A point of diminishing returns can be avoided if popular awareness drives a consistent motivation to conserve and respect the planet and its resources that gives humans life. As long as the First World has more incentives to partnership with the Third World, there will be less pressure for hegemonic exploitation and oppression of the poor. The world's monetary systems have for several decades been de-linked from the "gold standard." Many foreign currencies are linked to the stability of the U.S. Dollar. In reality, world trade flows between computers that track 1's and 0's, as the ledger between debits and credits. The Federal Reserve in collusion with international central banks can create money simply by adding zeros before the decimal point.

The strength of the world economy is in large part dependent on domestic and global confidence in the First World's (particularly the U.S.) ability to honor its currencies in exchange for technology, manufactured goods, and military assistance. In the hierarchy of the technological and commodities "food chain", the world's economy would collapse if the masses lost confidence in the purchasing value of western capital to buy "big ticket" items, such as ships, planes, tanks, manufacturing plants, and commercial computer systems, in addition to massive quantities of food and medicines that the west produces. The logical expectation is when a state's currency is honored for large top end items, it most certainly will support the daily purchases required to sustain comfortable lives on the lower levels through trickle down economics.

The North must remove the blinders of its avarice, and realize that the rest of the world depends in large part on the First World's economic vitality and humane leadership. The Third World has little desire to threaten (nor is it capable of such) the West, and instead desires to partnership with it, rather than to be its victim. Gradually raising the economic tide of the world over a generation can solve most of persistent global problems, and offers a greater opportunity for sustained peace. The world economic paradigm must necessarily change from one of competition and exploitation to one of partnership and exchange. Only then will the peoples and governments of the world realize sustained and effective cooperation to reduce population growth, and the negative impact of humans on the global environment; therefore providing a realistic platform for human progress and evolution while safeguarding the planetary ecosystem for future generations.

The First World hegemony, occupying the superior power position, can show greater wisdom beyond its greed, and take proactive steps to harness the abundance of our planet, rather than to view the world through the prejudicial and reality distorting filters of gloom and doom. It is the North that currently possesses the resources, capital, and technology to take the world *beyond conflict, violence, and war*. The orthodox zero-sum game paradigm is ruining the planet, nations, and directly or indirectly results in the genocide of Third World peoples. The question is, what will it take for the hegemon to adjust its operative policies and philosophical constructs to permit it to view the world and its great diversity in a more realistic and positive framework? The bottom line is whether or not the violent prone First World hegemony has the desire and will to bring true human rights to the world stage, beyond political rhetoric and positioning for selfish gains. The hopes of the world's population depend on a constructive reorientation of the North's role in the global community, from one of foe, to that of friend, and if the First World can see that's in its own interest, anything is possible. Conflict, violence, war, and extinction is not inevitable or certain.

References

Abernethy, Virginia, "Comment: The 'One World' Thesis as an Obstacle to Environmental Preservation," *Population and Development Review*, Vol. 16, Issue Supplement; "Resources, Environment, and Population: Present Knowledge, Future Options," (1990), 323-328.

Bland, Chester, and Dwight E. Lee, *Lectures in History* (Worcester, MA: Clark University Press, 1976).

Boot, John C. G., *Common Globe or Global Commons* (New York, NY: Marcel Dekker, 1974).

Brundtland, Gro Harlem, "Population, Environment, and Development." *Population and Development Review*, Vol. 19, Issue 4 (Dec., 1993), 893-899.

Chinese Delegation, "Chinese Statements on Population at Bucharest, 1974, and America City, 1984." *Population and Development Review*, Vol. 20, Issue 2 (Jun., 1994), 449-459.

Clinton, Richard L., William S. Flash, and R. Kenneth Godwin, *Political Science in Population*

Cohen, Joel E., "Should Population Projections Consider 'Limiting Factors" - and If So, How?" *Population and Development Review*, Vol 24, Issue Supplement: "Frontiers of Population Forecasting" (1998), 118.

Finkle, Jasor L., and Alisen McIntosh, "The New Politics of Population," *Population and Development Review*, Vol 20, Issue Supplement: "The New Politics of Population: Conflict and Consensus in Family Planning" (1994), 3-34.

Finnin, William M. Jr., and Gerald Alonzo Smith, Editors, *The Morality of Scarcity, Limited Resources and Social Policy* (Baton Rouge, LA: Louisiana State University Press, 1979).

Gilland, Bernard, "World Population, Economic Growth, and Energy Demand, 1990-2100: A Review of Projections," *Population and Development Review*, Vol. 21, Issue 3 (Sep., 1995), 507-539.

Grant, Lindsey, *Juggernaut, Growth on a Finite Planet* (Santa Ana, CA: Seven Locks Press, (1996)

Grimes, Kyle, "The Entropics of Discourse: Michael Harper's Debridement and the Myth of the Hero," *Black American Literature Forum*, Vol. 24, No. 3 (Autumn, 1990), pp. 417-440.

Hall, Christopher K., "The First Five Sessions of the UN Preparatory Commission for the International Criminal Court," *American Journal of International Law*, Vol. 94, No. 4 (Oct., 2000), pp. 773-789.

Hodgson, Dennis, "The Ideological Origins of the Population Association of America," *Population and Development Review*, Vol. 17, Issue 1 (Mar., 1991), 1-34.

Kasarda, John D., and Edward M. Crenshaw, "Third World Urbanization: Dimensions, Theories, and Determinants," *Annual Review of Sociology*, Vol. 17 (1991), 467-501.

Keohane, Robert O., "Hegemony in the World Political Economy," Reprinted by Permission in *International Politics*, 5 Edition, by Art, Robert J., and Robert Jervis, (New York, NY: Addison Wesley Longman, 2000).

Keyfitz, Nathan, "Population Growth, Development and the Environment," *Population Studies*, Vol. 50, Issue

3 (Nov., 1996), 335-359.

Keyfitz, Nathan, "Toward a Theory of Population-Development Interactions," *Population and Development Review*, Vol 16, Issue Supplement: "Resources, Environment, and Population: Present Knowledge, Future Options" (1990), 295-314.

Kremer, Michael Kremer, "Population Growth and Technological Change: One Million B.C. to 1990," *Quarterly Journal of Economics*, Volume 108, Issue 3 (Aug., 1993), 681-716.

LaRouche, Lyndon H. Jr., *Now, Are You Ready To Learn Economics?* (Washington D.C.: EIR News Service, Inc., 2000).

LaRouche, Lyndon H. Jr., *The Road To Recovery* (Leesburg, VA: New Bretton Woods, 1999).

Lubeck, Paul M., "The Crisis of African Development: Conflicting Interpretations and Resolution," *Annual Review of Sociology*, Vol. 18 (1992), 519-540.

Malkki, Liisa H., "Refugees and Exile: From "Refugee Studies" to the National Order of Things," *Annual Review of Anthropology*, Vol. 24 (1995), pp. 495-523.

McGeveran, William A. Jr., Ed., *The World Almanac and Book of Facts* 2001, (Mahwah, N.J.: World Almanac Books, 2001), pp. 372, 860.

Nagengast, Carole, "Violence, Terror, and the Crisis of the State," *Annual Review of Anthropology*, Vol. 23 (1994), pp. 109-136.

Neuhouser, Frederick, "Freedom, Dependency, and the General Will," *The Philosophical Review*, Volume 102, Issue 3 (Jul. 1993), pg. 363-395.

Olson, Mancur, "Mancur Olson on the Key to Economic Development," *Population and Development Review*, Vol. 24, Issue 2 (Jun., 1998), 369-379.

Olson, Mancur Jr., "Distinguished Lecture on Economics in Government: Big Bills Left on the Sidewalk: Why Some Nations are Rich, and Others Poor," *The Journal of Economic Perspectives*, Vol. 10, Issue 2 (Spring, 1996), 3-24.

Overbeek, Johannes, *The Population Challenge* (London, England: Greenwood Press, 1976).

Pasqualucci, Paolo, "Hobbes and the Myth of 'Final War.'" *Journal of the History of Ideas*, Vol. 51, Issue 4 (Oct.-Dec., 1990), 647-657.

Peterson, Paul E., "The Urban Underclass and the Poverty Paradox," *Political Science Quarterly*, Vol. 106, Issue 4 (Winter, 1991). (Peterson, 623)

Pope John Paul II, "Abortion, Contraception, and Euthanasia," *Population and Development Review*, Vol. 21, Issue 3 (Sep., 1995), 689-696.

Scott, John T., "The Theodicy of the Second Discourse: The 'Pure State of Nature' and Rousseau's Political Thought," *The American Political Science Review*, Volume 86, Issue 3 (Sep. 1992), pp. 696-711.

Shuger, Debora, "Irishmen, Aristocrats, and Other White Barbarians," *Renaissance Quarterly*, Vol. 50, No. 2 (Summer, 1997), pp. 494-525.

Singer, S. Fred, Editor, *Is There an Optimum Level of Population?* (N.Y.: McGraw-Hill, 1971).

Smith, Estellie M., "The Process of Sociocultural Continuity," *Current Anthropology*, Vol. 23, No. 2 (Apr., 1982), pp. 127-142.

Tapinos, Georges, and Phyllis T. Piotrow, *Six Billion People* (N.Y., NY: McGraw-Hill, 1978).

Waltz, Kenneth N., "The Anarchic Structure of World Politics," Reprinted with permission in *International Politics*, 5th Edition by Robert J. Art and Robert Jervis, (New York, NY: Addison Wesley Longman, 2000), pp. 49-51.

Weller, Robert H., and Leon F. Bouvier, *Population Demography and Policy* (New York, NY: St. Martin's Press, 1981).

Wilmoth, John, and Patrick Bal, "The Population Debate in American Popular Magazines, 1946-90." *Population and Development Review*, Vol. 18, Issue 4 (Dec., 1992), 631-668.

Yates, Wilson, *Family Planning on a Crowded Planet* (Minneapolis, MN: Augugsburg Publishing 1971).

The Political and Economic Imperative for a Global Population Control Strategy

The racist plan for global genocide of colored people hatched in 1974 by then Secretary of State "Deep Throat" Henry Kissinger and approved by President Gerald Ford a year later reflected the early thinking of the population control strategy subsequent to the publication of the book in 1968 entitled *The Population Bomb* by Paul Ehrlich that predicted a geometric increase in the global population to a tipping point where the Earth's resources would be insufficient to support the human population and there would ensue a catastrophic collapse of the world order. The report was originally prepared for President Richard Nixon, but the Watergate scandal derailed Nixon's paranoid ambitions and he was forced to resign in disgrace on August 9, 1974, almost 4 months prior to the day the global racist genocidal plot was issued. Following is the excerpt described on Wikipedia and retrieved on July 18, 2013, subject to its threatened removal.

National Security Study Memorandum 200: Implications of Worldwide Population Growth for U.S. Security and Overseas Interests (NSSM200) was completed on December 10, 1974 by the United States National Security Council under the direction of Henry Kissinger. It was adopted as official U.S. policy by President Gerald Ford in November 1975. It was originally classified, but was later declassified and obtained by researchers in the early 1990s.

The basic thesis of the memorandum was that population growth in the least developed countries (LDCs) is a concern to U.S. national security, because it would tend to risk civil unrest and political instability in countries that had a high potential for economic development. The policy gives "paramount importance" to population control measures and the promotion of contraception among 13 populous countries. This is to control rapid population growth that the US deems inimical to the socio-political and economic growth of these countries and to the national interests of the United States, since the "U.S. economy will require large and increasing amounts of minerals from abroad", and these countries can produce destabilizing opposition forces against the United States.

It recommends the US leadership to "influence national leaders" and that "improved world-wide support for population-related efforts should be sought through increased emphasis on mass media and other population education and motivation programs by the U.N., USIA, and USAID." Thirteen countries are named in the report as particularly problematic with respect to U.S. security interests: India, Bangladesh, Pakistan, Indonesia, Thailand, the Philippines, Turkey, Nigeria, Egypt, Ethiopia, America, Colombia, and Brazil. These countries are projected to create 47 percent of all world population growth.

The report advocates the promotion of education and contraception and other population control measures, stating for instance that "No country has reduced its population growth without resorting to abortion". It also raises the question of whether the U.S. should consider preferential allocation of surplus food supplies to states that are deemed constructive in use of population control measures.

Some of the key insights of report are controversial: "The U.S. economy will require large and increasing amounts of minerals from abroad, especially from less developed countries [see National Commission on Materials Policy, Towards a National Materials Policy: Basic Data and Issues, April 1972]. That fact gives the U.S. enhanced interest in the political, economic, and social stability of the supplying countries. Wherever a lessening of population pressures through reduced birth rates can increase the prospects for such stability, population policy becomes relevant to resource supplies and to the economic interests of the United States. . . . The location of known reserves of higher-grade ores of most minerals favors increasing dependence of all industrialized regions on imports from less developed countries. The real problems of mineral supplies lie, not in basic physical sufficiency, but in the politico-economic issues of access, terms for exploration and exploitation, and division of the benefits among producers, consumers, and host country governments" [Chapter III-Minerals and Fuel].

"Whether through government action, labor conflicts, sabotage, or civil disturbance, the smooth flow of needed materials will be jeopardized. Although population pressure is obviously not the only factor involved, these types of frustrations are much less likely under conditions of slow or zero population growth" [Chapter III-Minerals and Fuel]. "Populations with a high proportion of growth. The young people, who are in much higher proportions in many LDCs, are likely to be more volatile, unstable, prone to extremes, alienation and violence than an older population. These young people can more readily be persuaded to attack the legal institutions of the government or real property of the 'establishment,' 'imperialists,' multinational corporations, or other-often foreign-influences blamed for their troubles" [Chapter V, "Implications of Population Pressures for National Security].

"We must take care that our activities should not give the appearance to the LDCs of an industrialized country policy directed against the LDCs. Caution must be taken that in any approaches in this field we support in the LDCs are ones we can support within this country. "Third World" leaders should be in the forefront and obtain the credit for successful programs. In this context it is important to demonstrate to LDC leaders that such family planning programs have worked and can work within a reasonable period of time." [Chapter I, World Demographic Trends]

The report advises, "In these sensitive relations, however, it is important in style as well as substance to avoid the appearance of coercion." Abortion as a geopolitical strategy is mentioned several dozen times in the report with suggestive implications. These are some of the lines: "No country has reduced its population growth without resorting to abortion...under developing country conditions foresight methods not only are frequently unavailable but often fail because of ignorance, lack of preparation, misuse and non-use. Because of these latter conditions, increasing numbers of women in the developing world have been resorting to abortion..."

Subsequent to this report, the Chinese government first implemented a one-child policy in 1979 to curb its population growth when its population had reached 978 million by the end of 1978. Even with strict enforcement of the one child policy, China's population had reached 1.354 billion by the end of 2012, an increase of 376 million, or almost 40% increase over 34 years, roughly 1.2% per year. Had they permitted a 2 child policy, their population growth would have doubled to 752 million, and their 2013 population would now stand at 1.730 billion people, and at that rate would have added 41.5 million people each year to push their population to 2 billion people within 6 years, or by 2018. The socioeconomic implications of such unchecked population growth would have had a catastrophic effect on China's economic stability, and that in turn would have caused chaos in global markets, with dire implications for the United States of America.

People who doubt our government has contingency plans to deal with global population growth must have their heads buried in the sand because the global economy and viability of the ecosystem is directly related to population growth, which left unchecked could only exacerbate natural resource depletion and create a host of other challenges without clear answers. Anyone living during the Roaring 20's after Germany lost World War 1 would have thought anyone crazy were they to insist that Germany would rise again with imperialistic goals of conquering Europe and beyond. To suggest that a megalomaniac authoritarian ruler would in then their foreseeable future attempt to exterminate all Jews, gypsies, disabled, mentally ill and other humans deemed to be defective and inferior would invite ridicule, shock and disbelief. But it happened.

Now, genetic science and technology has place Homo sapiens on the precipice of a new world order, one in which the Orwellian vision will be pursued and great efforts will be made to cause its realization. The scientific, medical, and technological knowledge and tools already exist for revolutionary advances that is capable of artificially evolving the human species into something far exceeding current human capacities. What are some of these revolutionary techniques?

- Cloning was first accomplished with the sheep Dolly and only political, religious and scientific ethics prevent scientists from cloning people.
- Complete facial replacement was successfully done in 2012.
- Complete body transplantation is no more than 2 years away as a result of technological advancements in micro surgical instrumentation, equipment, techniques and procedures.
- Manipulation of stem cells for phenotypic expression has been achieved.
- Surrogate birthing is now commonplace among humans, and may be possible utilizing animal hosts in the very near future.
- Interspecies hybridization creates new subspecies such as Ligers, and were scientific ethics to become more liberal, other new hybridized species

can be created, perhaps Pegasus the flying horse, or pigs that can fly over the moon on a moonlit night.

- Xenotransplantation where organs from animals can be harvested for use in humans is not far off as the problems of rejection are overcome through stem cells and genetic manipulation techniques.

- Xeno-human hybridization is theoretically possible through genetic engineering once gene clusters are better understood and can be modified and adapted to permit interspecies compatibility. Perhaps the centaur is only a decade away. The artificial evolution of human beings into multiple new hybrid species is no longer ideas of science fiction writers, as it could be possible to improve the genetic composition of humans far beyond our wildest imagination to prepare our progeny for extensive space exploration.

- Immortality is not finding an external "fountain of youth" but rather discovering the gene clusters that control aging through the study of epigenetic functions and learning how to turn genes on and off.

Finally, science has caught up with eugenics. In the near future, expectant parents will be able to genetically design their progeny, far beyond the designer babies now being produced from sperm banks flouting the DNA of geniuses, athletes, musicians, and the wealthy. The natural next step after people gain control over their genetic reproductive choices will be the political movement to create perfect humans who are resistant to disease, are physically fit, resistant to environmental pollution, super intelligent and talented, emotionally stable, non-violent but fearless and heroic, and have a sense of humor, etc.

As these advances will occur first in First World developed nations, comprised primarily of white people, politicians will set forth legal standards to insure the eventual obsolescence of natural born humans as compared to GMOH's or genetically modified organism humans. To insure sufficient room and resources for the new species of advanced *Homo sapiens perfectio* or perfect human beings, a system of phasing out the old model of natural born humans will be implemented with specific standards and benchmarks with the eventual goal of limiting the human population to *2 billion people* with each natural death replaced by the advanced human model.

Eugenic Benchmarks

In order to make room for new human hybrid species that will be created to supply the mutants necessary for lengthy space travel and decreased impact on natural resources (who need a car if man can fly?), governments will institute a series of justifications to convince the populace of the necessity to phase out the existing old model *Homo sapiens.* Initially, the high cost of medical care will justify the government to withhold medical care from the aged, extremely ill, disabled and mentally ill to permit them to die off due to their deficiencies and insufficiencies.

In order to further reduce the world's population, performance benchmarks will be established, and those who meet the criteria will be allowed to live, and those who fail will be given a limited time before receiving humane euthanasia. A hypothetical scenario of the type of benchmarks might be the following:

Intelligence Parameters:
- A minimum I.Q. of 125 on Stanford-Binet Intelligence Test
- A Combined SAT score of 1100, with no score lower than 500 on either test
- College GPA. of 3.5 on 4.0 scale or High School GPA of 4.6 on 5.0 scale
- A Top 10 percentile score on at least one skill needed by global society: art, music, spatial, math, computer, speech, dance, game design, engineering, inventing, spiritual, or other practical aptitudes or skills.

Age Parameter: Children, and adults up to 60 years old, meeting the criteria:
- MRI indicates no internal disease or damage to skeletal or organ structures
- DNA test indicates no genetic defects or predisposition to disease
- B.P. under 140/90 on empty stomach, after ½ hour sedentary, prone period
- Body fat not to exceed 20%, and weight not to exceed 30% of Y2K body type standards
- No STDs or history of dormant or incurable STDs
- No history of drug or alcohol abuse or convictions
- No history of psychological or psychiatric problems

- No history of violence
- No functional disabilities (excepted as below)

All persons must meet the minimum benchmarks on an annual basis and pass an array of physical, mental, emotional and knowledge/skills/talent tests to renew their permission to live. Failure to pass benchmarks subjects individuals to a one-year probationary period requiring monthly testing and evaluation. Failure to pass benchmarks after the probation period subjects the individual to euthanasia.

Exception to 60-year-old rule:

- Individual possesses skills required for species advancement in science, art, technology, spirituality, philosophy, music, invention, engineering, computers, or other fundamental areas of knowledge deemed necessary for species survival or space travel.

- Individual possesses monetary or convertible hard assets (discounting paper wealth such as stocks) exceeding 100 times the global average per capita income pegged to Y2K (estimated at $100,000 U.S.) adjusted for inflation.

- The political, military, and economic elites may have blood relations exempted from meeting minimal requirements and will be allowed to live out natural lives up to 60 years of age; however, all such persons exempted will not be allowed to procreate.

Procreation:

1. Age Limit = 30; Limited to 1 child
2. Exceptions: Global government determines areas of genetic diversity deficiency on annual basis, and issues permits to couples or surrogate singles to have specific genotype offspring deemed necessary to species survival and advancement.
3. The goal is to keep world population at about 2 billion people, at whatever means necessary.
4. All minimal intelligence and physical ability criteria must be met by parents.

Immortality:

Eligible for cloned bodies and cerebral transplantation:

1. Individuals who attain MENSA status (top 2% of population)
2. Individuals who perform physical tasks at top 5% of population, i.e. sports

and stamina

3. Individuals possessing skills and talents per exceptions above
4. Individuals possessing assets per exceptions above
5. Individuals who are deemed "beautiful" by global order (top 1% of population like Kate Upton)

Impending pervasiveness of "Big Brother" to monitoring the ideas, activities and location of the global human population – the timeline

1980s: Robotics introduced to auto building assembly lines

1990s: Cell phone explosion, Voice recognition email, Proliferation of ISPs and free email

2000: Interactive voice recognition phone trees, PCs increase processing speed by a factor of 40 times within 10 years; chip memory quadruples, Data transmission speed limited to bipolar metal wire molecular structure, and the Dotcom crash

2010: First World optical fiber network in place and secured, Data transmission speed increase by 1000x due to optic fiber network. Voice recognition linked to robotic equipment, Integrated "Watchman" nano-computers and smart phones with GPS wireless telecommunication, Bio-computer microchip linked to GPS, real time data storage and retrieval, with built in automatically scanned "walk-in, walk-out" purchasing software

2020: You can run, but you can't hide. The repeal of privacy laws, and installation of the "Big Brother" microchip to everyone

The Global Order Hierarchy

Highest Tier: USA – Germany – Britain – Canada – Australia – Japan – China

Second Tier: Russia – France – Western Europe – Israel – Developed Asia

Third Tier: Developing Asia – Latin America – America – Middle East

Bottom Tier: Africa – All undeveloped and Impoverished Nations

Future Developments Leading to the New World Order

Political

1. U.S. Hegemony
2. German Hegemonic Goals
3. Demise of Britain
4. China's Balancing Act
5. Russian Resurgence
6. Rise of Islamic Extremism
7. Domestic & Global Terrorism
8. Other Significant Global Actors
9. Politics of Oil Supply Manipulation
10. Political & Bureaucratic Reform
11. Environmental Impact

Economic

1. Oil & Energy Market Manipulation
2. Stock Market Manipulation
3. Corporate Corruption
4. Effects of Bureaucratic Reform
5. Internet Commerce
6. Corporate Downsizing
7. Unemployment Pandemic
8. Acts of Terrorism
9. Environmental Impact

Social

1. Mass Media Manipulation
2. Educational Reforms
3. Bifurcation of Classes
4. Feminist Agenda
5. Racial Politics
6. Political Agenda

7. Civic Capital

8. Privacy & Spying

9. Government Controls & Laws

10. Cloning and Genetic Modifications

Science & Technology

1. Computer Technology Advancements

2. Genetic Engineering

3. Bio-Technology Advancements

4. Energy Technology Advancements

5. Robotics Advancements and Applications

6. Spying Technology Pervasiveness

7. Space Exploration

8. Deep Ocean Exploration

9. Planetary Deterioration

10. Near Space Objects

Religious

1. Conflict and Confluence with Scientific Knowledge

2. Resistance to Substantive Change

3. Inter-religious Conflict

4. Extraterrestrial Contacts

5. Discovery of method to measure the existence of "the soul"

Predictions

1. Political

2. Economic

3. Social

4. Science & Technology

5. Religious

6. Extraterrestrials

Conclusions

1.   Globalization
2.   Secret World Government
3.   Extraterrestrial Collusion
4.   Self-Fulfilling Prophecy
5.   The Final Conflict

Implementing The New World Order Timeline

The history of the world has always been the struggle for dominance between the powerful and the relatively powerless. A dynamic life and death balance occurs at all levels of life, from viruses to humans, just as it had once existed among dinosaurs and earliest life. Is mankind's problems part of natural selection? Has the hand of divine intervention been no more than an innate human desire for benevolent paternalism? And if so, is the human desire to believe in gods or a monotheistic God based on a psychological fear of the harsh environment that has always been naturally filled with violence and danger over time? And if there is such an superior intelligent entity as God, why should that presumption exclude the existence of lesser gods, defined as intelligent living beings who are superior to humans? If God exist, why isn't it at least probable that humans have been, continue to be, and will in the future be visited by gods, not all of whom want to embrace and love humans, but rather to dominate us, as in the past?

Simple math and science relative to cosmology indicates that the earth is no more than 5.5 billion years old, orbiting a lesser star, the sun, in the outer quadrant of the Milky Way, a lesser galaxy in the outer quadrant of a visible universe that is 12-15 billion years old. Primates that may be relatives to humans appeared on earth about a mere 4.5 million years ago. The visible universe contains over 100 billion billion galaxies, each containing over 100 billion stars. We are infants in the scope of time, in the breath of life. Once again, our ethnocentrism tries to justify that we are the center of intelligent life, yet human history and contemporary affairs has repeatedly proven that we are not very intelligent, and definitely not particularly wise or humane as a species. What other

111

species makes it a routine activity to kill its own kind in massive numbers, and to exterminate millions of other species, whether deliberately or inconsiderately?

Viewed from space, humans are like a disease, overrunning and killing everything, animals, plants, and the ecosystem. And we feel justified, a manifest destiny to spread our need to explore and dominate into space, to other planets. And what will humans likely do, should we finally figure out how to get "there"? Probably the same program as we have on Earth. Plunder, exploit, extract, destroy, and kill anything that gets in the way, just as the program against the 3rd World has been effected since Europe's boom days in exploration led to imperialism, colonialism, neo-colonialism, and now globalization. How close we are to global thermal nuclear war is a subject of debate and secret preparations by paranoid governments who attempt to protect their assets from other states and "terrorists." Perhaps the smallest life forms, the bacteria will reclaim the Earth from humans, by catastrophic plague from which no known anti-biotic is effective. That might be a good thing for the planet, though not good for *Homo sapiens.*

Since the development of city-states evolved into nation-states, various forms of government were created to give dominance and economic advantage to elite classes of humans. In the quest and justification for social order and peace, states have gone to war thousands of times, killing over a billion people over time. Empires, kingdoms, and dynasties still exist, but in modern form, renamed with more eloquent terms, like democracy and socialism. The elite 10% of humans still own or control 90% of the land and resources of our planet, and in too many cases, that includes ownership of human beings as slaves, serfs, and indentured servants who are exploited at low wages, for crime, or prostitution to enrich the coffers of their "employers". No matter what nation we look, the game is the same, only the names change.

The rich exploit the poor. The poor are too busy trying to survive meager lives to organize for better rights, as they have become sheep, afraid of the wolves, the police, para-military, and military whose primary job is to protect the equity owners in their respective nations, not to protect people. Only a fool would feel more secure when as a commercial jetliner passenger, one sees the jet fighter escorts off its wing tips. The escorts' job is to shoot down the commercial jet, should there "appear" to be a threat the jet will be used instead as a bomb. Suicidal "terrorists" or deranged individuals care little if they are killed in the course of acting out their agenda against the public, and a glorified death is their primary goal.

If the role of military jets is now to shoot down commercial jets, then every passenger should be issued parachutes and briefed on their use as part of boarding and emergency information dispensed by flight attendants. But that would cost too much for airlines. Once again, a price has been placed on human life, so the common religious thought that human life is precious and priceless is a lie, otherwise its followers would practice that value. The scientists are probably more realistic in stating that a human being's trace elements are worth less than ten dollars in carbon compounds. Or maybe a convicted felon from a Chinese prison is worth the cost of his transplantable parts, which to that convict or political prisoner becomes a negative incentive, worth a couple of hundred dollars to the state.

And now, we have a czar of homeland security in America. We should know that any bureaucracy that has been created is likely to grow, to usurp more power, and to jealously guard their jurisdiction. The history of organizational behavior indicate that its actors will refuse to relinquish power and budget, once its been given. What will the evolution of homeland security become? Will citizens be required to organize "building watch", "school watch", and "job watch" as a more pervasive and ominous form of current day voluntary "neighborhood watch"? How did the "SS" begin in pre-WW2 Germany? Perhaps citizens, for "their own protection" will be required to carry "national identification cards", a "smart-card" with intrusive personal, financial, and medical information, encoded and assessable only to banks, insurance companies, and the government. And what logically comes after the "smart card"? GPS micro chip implants?

We need to look no further than recent history to see the effects of both state-sponsored proactive terrorism, mass-based reactive terrorism, and individually-based Kamikaze terrorism. The seeds of rebellion and terrorism have been planted by state-sponsored or supported terrorism that is the common legacy of imperialism, colonialism, neo-colonialism, and corrupt regimes. There are no "truly innocent" parties, and no "true victims" in acts of terrorism. Neither non-

113

combatants nor military personnel can claim neutrality. To the degree that they benefit, even those who benefit, however slightly, from the economic, political, and military policies of states that oppress other peoples, is in a way complicity "not innocent" of the consequences of such policies, and is "not innocent" of the logical and predictable consequences and rebellion that invariably and inevitably result as desperate reactions to oppression and great disparities.

So how is the world going to get out of this latest round of terrorism? Will "smoking out terrorist", and "getting them on the run" truly solve the root causes of terrorism? Or will harsh military and economic policies and disparate globalization serve to galvanize a new and even deadlier generation of suicidal religious zealots. The "kill" ratio of 19 terrorist was about 6,000 in the WTC incident of 9-11-01. If that rate can be sustained by 1,900 terrorist, then 600,000 people would be killed. If 19,000 terrorists, 6,000,000 people could die (the same number of people murdered during the Holocaust). If 190,000 terrorists, 60,000,000 people could be killed. But we're only talking about flying jets into skyscrapers. Bio-terrorism or nuclear terrorism would undoubtedly up the ante and "kill ratio". Maybe that's part of the plan.

The survival of mankind will depend on fundamentally changing the elitist global system that supports and enforces the grossly inequitable distribution of economic resources to the great suffering of the poor. But will the rich voluntarily give up their power and wealth? Never. But might the elites consider paradigm changes if it could be proven that their short term, and especially long-term need for social and political stability could be better served by changing specific facets of the world system? Possibly.

Impending global paradigm changes can be seen on the event horizon that will alter the manner in which humans related to each other, and how nation-states deal with the global village, and its own domestic affairs. The possible outcomes are many, and the extreme consequences could either be human extinction, or human enlightenment, nuclear and genetic war killing billions of people, or consensual interaction and engagement leading to long lasting peace and prosperity for all. Or there may be "external" extraterrestrial forces that will create a complete realignment of human perceptions and values, whether that would be in the form of an "Armageddon" sized asteroid or returning of the "gods", no one

114

can predict. We shall know, when we can know.

The impending paradigm changes are many, cross several disciplines, and will invariably have interactive effects on almost all aspects of life. Elitism versus powerlessness has been institutionalized and woven into cultures as class, racism, ethnic bias, religious intolerance, and sex has resulted in great suffering and poverty for exploited and debased people. Governance and organizational structure and power has been hierarchical, centralized, and unequal instead of decentralized, horizontally multi-tiered, and consensual that encourages power sharing instead of concentration. The world economic system is based on pure profit, with little or no regards for resource depletion or inhumane human exploitation and disparities.

The elites' vision of a completely integrated global market, controlled by a relatively small group of MNC's, owned by a handful of elites, who in collusion control every nation-state on the planet, is a twisted idea based on wanton greed and profiteering from other peoples' grief. It is unclear at what point the masses will rebel, or whether they may acquiesce to authority, as in the United States. It is unclear if the elites will someday unleash their technological and military might to kill 5-6 billion poor and non-white people, to "cleanse" the world of poverty, defects, violence, and procreation leaving a world with a dichotomy, those inhabitants who rule, and those who purpose is to serve those who rule.

Technological advances are even now pushing the envelope in science and will impact global social, political, military and economic systems in a wide range of areas within the next decade. New sources of renewable energy, genetic manipulation, "clean" weapons of mass destruction, extra-low-frequency (ELF) mind-control methods, climatic disruptions or control, and space exploration will pressure the status quo to adjust and to integrate the impending changes into their global system of profiteering. Will the result be greater control on the minds, hearts, and souls of human beings? Or will something better emerge? I hope the later, but if history is a teacher, then I fear the former. Let's hope for a quantum improvement in the quality of life, with an increase in purposefulness, and a de-emphasis on materialism and consumerism. Let's pray for peace and stability through education and empowerment, to avoid more violence.

Perplexing questions abound about globalization:

1.   Where does the world stand now? Most societies remain relatively racially homogeneous where European nations are predominantly white, reflecting specific ethnic groups such as Russian, German, English, Irish, Swede or whatever. Primarily "yellow" skinned people populate Asian nations, while Latin American and Middle-East nations primarily consist of "brown" skinned individuals and Africa by "black" skinned people. The world is racially divided by continents due to migration and natural selection. Globalization is primarily a racially exploitative economic strategy of the manipulated capitalistic market system that takes resources from lands occupied by non-white peoples and pay low wages to non-white laborers to manufacture goods for consumers in predominantly white nations.

2.   Who and what groups are behind it? The wealthy global power elites own most of the world's land (including 3rd World autocrats) and resources while commoners are relatively poor. Developed nations, primarily in Europe and parts of Asia have significant middle class buffers between the rich and the poor, otherwise the socioeconomic paradigm in most developing nations is bifurcated between extreme wealth and abject poverty. Even in 3rd World nations, lighter skinned people are usually given higher social status than darker skinned individuals because it denotes less exposure to sunlight, which means a higher occupational status as compared to working outside.

3.   Who stands to gain and who will lose? As long as market based capitalism is based upon a zero sum game plan, where ideally, the least amount of goods is sold for the highest possible price subject to supply and demand forces, again the owners of natural resources and the means of production will continue to benefit while consumers will be subjected to recurring price fluctuations.

4.   Structural changes and pre-conditions.

5.   Is globalization good for humanity?

6.   Despots, democracy, or destruction?

7.   How could globalization benefit everyone?

Let's discuss the accelerated developments in the globalization game. The pre-conditions, pros and cons, and probable scenarios, consequences, and outcomes will be explored. Material will be presented to identify who (which groups) stand to benefit the most economically and politically from globalization. We will also describe certain structural changes that will signal the onset and configuration of globalization that is not too far off in our developing future.

Let's discuss the facts and trends:

1. Evaluation of current degree and breadth of globalization.
2. MNC's, elites, trade brokers, governments, secret international organizations), NGO's.
3. The elites versus the poor.
4. Economic, political, cultural, religious, and environmental impact of globalization.
5. Efficient and effective global distribution versus hoarding and exploitation.
6. New World Order, the UN, diplomacy, world vision, and the ultimate military options.
7. An ideal world, happiness, peace, and global cooperation is a potential reality.

The world system and global economic order based on a bifurcated capitalistic system where the top ten percent of people own and/or control 80% of global resources creates and reinforces many inequities that result in the preventable suffering and deaths of millions of innocent people each year. It would be more beneficial for all classes and races of people were the rich and powerful to understand that providing abundance to all people regardless of race, class, nationality and regionalism create ample opportunities to magnify the existing wealth of the elites many folds as the rising tide lifts all boats.

Furthermore, as technology and more efficient techniques are developed to farm the world's minerals and natural resources, replacing deforestation, water pollution, fossil fuels with new terra farming, harnessing the oceans and wave motions, lightening collection farming, more efficient wind and solar energy, more energy efficient vehicles and appliance, and improved methods for water conservation and desalinization, there should be no reason anyone in the world must be underfed, denied adequate medical care, or allowing able bodied people to work in newly spawned industries that robots haven't taken over.

Conspiracy theorists have promoted New World Order scenarios for the past decade, concluding that globalization, the rise of oligarchies, and the computer-technology explosion are the means through which the singular world government will come about. Juxtaposed against the one world order paradigm is American hegemony and military might, as the sole remaining "superpower" in the world.

Let's examine the logic, evidence and motivation behind the creation of a singular world government. Let's explore the probable answers to the essential questions that must be resolved before credibility should be attributed to the global empire paradigm.

1.   Why would any individual, group, nation, or ethnic group desire to rule the world, with all of its problems, conflicts and turmoil? What are historical precedents and reasons for empire building and world domination?

2.   If it were possible for any one individual, group, race, ethnicity, or nation to rule the world, how could they accomplish such an enormous and complex feat?

3.   What individuals, groups, or nations could have the desire to rule the world? Who might they be, why, and why during our modern era?

4.   What individuals, groups, or nations actually possess the potential resources, economic, political and military power that would be required to rule the world?

5.   Of those with such awesome potential power, desire and capability, which individuals, groups, or national leaders would most likely be the ones to attempt world domination and world rule?

6.   What obstacles could prevent the creation of a singular world ruler or government?

7.   What aspects of a centralized world government could be beneficial to humanity, which aspects would be destructive, and in what ways.

8. How could the power of a centralized world government be abused?

9. What international safeguards can be put in place to prevent abuse of global economic, political, and military power?

10. What technological safeguards should be put in place to prevent global thermal nuclear war, or limited nuclear war, should a singular world ruler or government eventually have dominion over all the nations of the world?

The answer to these questions will greatly clarify the potential effects of globalization, as a means toward creating a centralized world government.

The Need to Exercise Ethical Principles in the Halls of the Powerful Elites

An exploration of the spirit of public service presumes that the intention and practice of serving others are inherently good and beneficial to the development and maintenance of civil societies that seek to maximize individual liberties and happiness, within the context of normative moral codes of conduct. Rousseau theorized in his construction of the "civil society" viewed morals as that which is "established" by "a sort of convention" as men begin to associate together, and a "political" form that is moral in the sense of being "authorized" by the consent of man as a social contract (Scott, 1992). Neuhouser (1993) elaborates on Rousseau, by stating, If the general will (and the laws derived from it) expresses a consciously shared concept of the common good that is affirmed by the individuals who make up the state, then submitting to laws that derive from the general will subjects individuals only to their own wills, and therefore they remain tree.... The general will must regulate social cooperation in accord with the common good and at the same time be the will of the individuals whose behavior it governs; thus individuals can achieve freedom through the general will only if the general will is also their own will (Neuhouser, 1993).

The implications of building civil societies are the active and responsible consensus among citizens to seek societal improvement as fundamentally desirable and requisite goals. The presumption of mutual good is aptly described by the cliché, "the rising tide raises all ships", and consequently in order to raise the level of benefit for all, substantive and effective efforts must focus on systemic factors such as structural and philosophical change, which in turn guides the thought, motivation, and actions of individuals, who as a collective contribute to a rising tide.

Were individuals to be left to their own selfish designs, would the propensity for greed and hoarding tend to outpace compassion and humanitarianism, and contribute to societal decay, decline, and possible anarchy? The history of mankind has provided ample lessons about social and political disorder, conflict, violence and war, not as the outcome of individual competition, but rather as the design of madmen, despots, regimes, and states. It is clear that governments, and those actors who lead and benefit most from manipulating the masses, are more inclined to affect the public welfare, whether for good or otherwise. The biographies of uniquely proactive individuals, whose visions and abilities enabled them to overcome obstacles, demonstrate that through political, social, and economic networks, which provide platforms to influence the decisions of high government leaders and officials on issues of public service, reveal that a rare few humans have achieved the level of spiritual and humanitarian enlightenment to deserve immortality. Among those elect few can be counted the likes of Jane Adams and Clara Barton.

It is clear that public service is the usual path to cause social change by increments, where honest ethical and non-corrupt public servants encourage public trust and enhance achievements in the public's best interest. As population growth increases competing interests, public servants (whether official or non-governmental) are forced to balance highly dynamic social orders, where intergroup and individualistic conflicts compete for limited resources and create unpredictable and potentially volatile climates. As globalization advances, societies more pressed to universally accept the proliferation of scientific orientation, technological advances, state secrecy and a capitalist paradigm where the "ends justifies the means", as the minimum ticket for survival. Personal, organizational, and governmental responsibilities and liabilities have become mired in complex webs of conflict that require lengthy, exhaustive and wasteful expenditures of resources. Incidents of brute force to solve complex situations appear to becoming more the rule than the exception as the number of global military conflicts has dramatically escalated since World War II.

Several common character traits are shared by renowned humanitarians, among which were high intelligence, a strong drive to achieve, and most importantly, a lifelong commitment to particularly purposeful public service causes. Adams, Mulholland, Moses, and Nightingale all demonstrated their lifelong commitment to public service. African-American Dr. Martin Delany, who was a Renaissance Man; a dentist, writer, editor, medical doctor, theorist, abolitionist, explorer, scientist, philosopher, diplomat, civil rights activist, ethnologist, and politician, and during the Civil War, an army major, surgeon, and recruiter. Delany is paid tribute particularly for his vigor and mastery of these professions in his mission to strive toward the restoration, reclamation, redevelopment, and enhancement of African people's lives (Ogunlele, 1998).

Several common characteristics were apparent among the majority of biographies presented in class, among which were the privileged opportunities available in networks of actors and elites that influenced politically and economically powerful people, who gave support to individuals with visionary ideas and projects. Another historical-political observation is that certain great events during an era give rise to extraordinary achievements and people. In the case of Moses, Liliental, and Soper, major paradigm shifts in society responding to exceptional public challenges and technological advances facilitated major change and accomplishments that might not have otherwise been possible regardless of the abilities and persistence of individuals. A few of the biographies discussed in class were born of humble beginnings, who through hard work, determination, creativity, and people skills, convinced others with power to support their visions. More typical were those born into the privileged classes, which came with a natural placement in empowering personal and professional environments, even in the cases where gender restrictions were in place. Each of the biographies disclosed character traits of sincere selflessness and strong desire to benefit others. Their spirit for public service elevated and drove their missions to the status of noble and worthwhile undertakings that could garner both political and public support intertwined with elitist philanthropic motivations.

Case Study Examples

Tenet Healthcare, a Fortune 100 corporation, is the second largest operator of privately-owned hospitals in the United States, providing medical services for a handsome profit. The complex billing structure utilized by giant corporations such

121

as Tenet has created an environment where allegations of discrimination, unfair practices, and fraud eventually surface to public awareness. Even after many years of accumulated irregularities and potential violations of fair practices or legal statutes, rarely are corrections made until whistleblowers are able to raise public consciousness and ire.

A class action lawsuit was recently filed against St. Luke's Medical Center, and Tenet Healthcare Corporation for alleged discriminatory pricing against persons of Hispanic heritage (Oskin, 2002). Under the previous name of N.M.E., National Medical Enterprises, who previously paid a substantial fine ten years ago for other unethical and irregular business practices, appears to continue similar business practices that got them into trouble with regulators in the past. As part of the settlement with the government, a consent decree mandated all N.M.E./Tenet employees to undergo annual "ethics training", which unfortunately exempts the top executives who actually set corporate fiscal and operational policies.   On paper, Tenet's ethics program is very impressive, with presentations that discuss hypothetical case studies, and presenters who espouse high ideals.

And while the great preponderance of employees appear to adhere to ethical practices; corporate policy makers appear to project a public image of high ethics, but to practice much less. Proponents of NPM, New Public Management, should examine the cases of Tenet, along with Enron, PG&E, Edison Int'l, Tyco, and other major providers of public services, whether health care, energy, or whatever. Does the rush to privatization and contracting with the private sector actually provide a more cost-effective service delivery system, or perhaps only greater opportunities for profit, conflict of interests, fraud and abuse? As a former employee of Tenet Healthcare, I surmise the jury is still out on this and other major corporations whose profits depend on providing services in the public domain, often with little scrupulous consideration of the public good and without the spirit of public service, as they focus on the pursuit of profit.

The second example chronicles significant public services that Stacy provides as a credible and reliable FBI informant, whose secret testimonies have landed corrupt law enforcement officials and criminals in jail. The FBI was able to obtain information from wiretaps on several of her close acquaintances, whose phone numbers were obtained from her phone bills. Her acquaintances, friends, and family are routinely "probed" by mysterious callers who appear to be "fronts" for law enforcement or certain criminal organizations who attempt to ascertain Stacy's whereabouts and associations.

Not unlike many of the persons discussed in class, Stacy is a courageous person. She was overheard in a taped conversation stating, "You fluking guys are so stupid! You sent some guys to "whack" me, but instead, those horny guys fell in love with me, and couldn't whack such a pretty girl as me. You fluking [ethnic slur] would sell your own mothers for a chance to get into my pants. If you guys keep being so nosy about people I know, I'm gonna put you guys away for twenty years!" If standing up for justice in the face of death threats and attempts without FBI protection or personal bodyguards takes "guts", then she certainly has raw courage.

Has Stacy demonstrated the "spirit of public service?" Certainly there are less corrupt officials and criminals on the streets (arguably over 100). Did she personally benefit, or were her actions selfless? Stacy revealed that she has never sought, nor was she ever offered or paid one cent of reward money for her disclosures. She is an unsung hero, whose personal crusade against corruption and crime depicts a true and uninhibited spirit of public service no less than those heroes who serve our nation and people daily in the military, in public safety, or in other areas for the public good, at substantial risks and sacrifice of their personal safety. When asked why she places herself at risk, she responded, "I hate corrupt officials who work with criminals to rip people off." In terms of motivation for public service, that passion is no less valid or noble than a desire to find a cancer cure.

Improving the quality of public officials is an issue that is gaining greater public and political awareness. Do those who are motivated to draw on their government experience and stature for private gain serve the public interest best? Stark opined that the public is not best served by officials who, are motivated to spend more time working on certain files, cultivating certain kinds of contacts, and devote more energy to acquiring certain kind of reputation, than they would were they less concerned to use their time in office to develop marketable skills and capacities (Stark, 1997).

Contributing to the temptation for some in public service to enhance their own marketability is the lure of post-public employment opportunities created by the push to reinvent government by adopting "new public management" strategies such as privatization. Durant raises fundamental questions on the basic premise of private sector superiority to deliver public services.... But are market-based approaches to service delivery do more with less, more effectively, and in the public interest than did government bureaucracies prior to privatization? Or do they as critics claim, only produce the worst of both worlds, leading to lower efficiency, quality, employee security, and public accountability? (Durant, 1998).

The push to balance government budgets at all levels has contributed to a retrenchment from public service. Wilson (1996) opined that, "as spending on social programs decreases, the growth of joblessness and welfare receipt mainly reflect a declining commitment to the core values of society" (Wilson, 1996). Many public officials have become frustrated by the apparent inability of the legislative process to accommodate non-partisan views, as indicated by a significant number who leave the House of Representatives because they didn't feel the structure allowed them to promote policies they personally support (Moore, 1998). While some politicians lose their spirit of public service, and are either voted out, or voluntarily resign, the bureaucracy provides ample opportunity for the exercise of individual judgment and policy-making. Coleman (1998) describes the dilemma of bureaucratic decision-making authority:

The delegation of policy-making authority to the administrative agencies of government poses a fundamental dilemma in democratic societies. On the one hand, administrative discretion is essential since legislators can not anticipate all of the possible circumstances that may arise in the applications of public laws. As a result, bureaucrats are asked to draw upon their experience, expertise, judgment, and intuition to make administrative decisions. But on the other hand, public administrators lack accountability at the ballot box, and civil service regulations designed to prevent political manipulation shield them from elected officials, as their specialization, expertise, and clientele support constrain the ability of political officials to control bureaucratic action (Coleman, 1998).

It is ironic that many elected officials called upon to represent "the people" lose their desire to serve the public, from frustration or desire to profit from their public service repertoire and connections by hiring on with the private sector. Both politicians and bureaucrats have often become manipulators of public sentiment, rather than sincerely serving the public good. Often, simply by coining new words, or by eloquent but confusing explanations of intent, public servants are able to present their personal slant on public service, under the guise of public benefit. Chabot (1995) referred to Montaigne, a Thomas Hobbes contemporary, who opined that euphemisms of language "could any longer evaluate the fairness of its conduct or the sincerity of its motives. Viciousness donned the cloak of righteousness. Ambition had become courage, stubbornness masquerading as piety, and behind every diplomatic overture there lurked a blasphemous heart (Chabot, 1995). It is unlikely that the sincere spirit of public service exemplified by the lives of public spirited individuals such as Perkins, Delany, and Adams would allow the degradation of the public good, without issuing vehement social and political protest and sacrificing their lives to positive social and political change.

A review of biographical and historical material, scholars' views, case studies, and philosophical aspects of public service provides a rich tapestry of diversity and individualism focused on benefiting the greater common good. If we see a future vision of prosperity, cooperation, and humanity, we will likely achieve it. If we see a future of chaos and warfare, we will probably focus our limited resources on preparing for the next war, and perhaps even the "final war" to end all wars, the one that might bring the end to human existence. What societies collectively view as probable future scenarios is what human beings are likely to receive, if for no other reason than the self-filling prophecy. Political leaders need to describe a clearer vision of the type of future that humans need, want, and are capable of achieving.

If unregulated capitalism is allowed to reinforce and advance highly racially disparate realities between the rich and the poor, instead of becoming a positive driving force for advancing all human beings while preserving the global environment, then we can expect more accelerated outcomes that lead to greater degrees of conflict, violence, and war. The universal purpose of wealth building should be to fulfill humanitarian missions that provide improvements to service human needs in health care, education, infrastructure, environment, science, arts, music, space exploration, and elevating the human spirit, morals and civility. Media and marketing should change their focus from creating illusions that create artificial needs like cosmetics, to public service that addresses the real needs of people, such as health care, food, and shelter.

Why can't media and business promote new worthwhile competitive "sports" that include equal access and contributions of both men and women on the same teams, where something productive is accomplished besides placing another ball through another hole. How about teams who compete to build the best houses in the shortest period of time, or who clean a mile of beach front in the fastest time? Why not propose a game where children are taught new skills, then compete to demonstrate their competence in applying those skills, for example in designing and building a simple robot? In this way, we can elevate the desirability of accomplishing things that benefit the public good, and are not simply escapist activities that benefit the relatively few professional team owners or competitors.

Unfortunately, human civilizations have been mired in exploiting the masculine dominance paradigm at the great disadvantage of females and societies in general. Gender insecurities are reinforced by media advertising to create markets for clothes, cars, cosmetics, and "crappy" products, where buying "name brands" translates to higher profits with little or no appreciable value added for consumers. Why not create genderless markets that instill the love of community, environment, and public service, where all interested people could participate, regardless of sex, race, age, disability, ethnicity, culture or religion? Do we really need another "awards" show to celebrate "celebrities"? How about awards shows that celebrate the best that each occupation has produced; the best teachers, carpenters, fishers, farmers, police, parents, and so on?

Until societies can celebrate reality instead of illusions, then our combined destinies will likely remain stuck on superficialities while the real problems of the world continue to be ignored, compounded, and exacerbated until perhaps it's too late. The spirit of public service demands that leadership, resources, and public awareness be focused on dealing with reality, and not in illusory escapism from the real world. When the capitalism paradigm shifts from profiting on illusion creation and fulfillment, to profiting from real world problems resolution, then humans will witness their greatest period of advancement, far beyond what even the Renaissance Period had produced.

Let the spirit of public service push us forward into an era of peace and enlightenment, and away from the dismal dichotomy of global exploitation of the poor, females, and color peoples. Let the spirit of public service build better and more civil societies for all. I believe that an engaged citizen is one who loves his nation and cherishes his family and community, and demonstrates desire to improve life for others. Americans are the global leaders by default, for good and for bad, and it behooves our leaders and residents to try to improve the conditions of our nation and the world.

Biographies of great achievers and leaders indicate that a prerequisite of vision, powerful connections, public support, and persistence set apart the enduring "doers" from the lot. History also has shown that the social and political climate must be ripe for change, in order for positive change to occur. The world may be within such an opportune moment in evolving history, to seize the momentum to push for rapid positive changes through the cooperation and support of elite capitalists and political leaders to push for a kinder, gentler, more responsible, and more humanitarian and environmentally sensible form of capitalism.   Society needs desperately to change cultural socialization to eliminate concepts that cause inequality, exploitation, and violence, thereby creating a more civil society. Thirdly, public service is called upon to create environments where every human being can pursue happiness through appropriate infrastructure support, institutional equity, structural fairness, and the exercise of personal conscience to do what's right and in the best interest of the public good.

Human beings can make the world a better place, except that it will required the leadership and support of elite actors. The "zero-sum game" paradigm continues to dictate perceptual reality and the distorted paradigms upon which most socialized people based their beliefs and actions. Social construction has created a set of mirrors that provides a distorted view of reality, and until global leaders choose to look beyond their insular biases, and view the human race and planet Earth as one interrelated biosphere, then little change can take place. The world is what the human collective makes it, for better or for worse. People who justify the exploitation of others through dishonesty and corruption may obtain substantial material and monetary gains during their lifetimes, but the cost to the human species is likely to be paid by future generations whose survival may be jeopardized by the unethical behavior and strategies of greedy people in the present.

References

Chabot, Dana, 1995. "Thomas Hobbes: skeptical moralist", *The American Political Science Review*, Vol. 89, Issue 2 (June, 1995), 401-410. Retrieved from the World Wide Web, March 1, 2002 from http://www.jstor.org.

Coleman, Sally, Jeffrey L. Brucney, and J. Edward Kellough, 1998. "Bureaucracy as a representative institution; toward a reconciliation of bureaucratic government and democratic theory", *American Journal of Political Science*, Vol. 42, Issue 3 (July, 1998), 717-744. Retrieved from the World Wide Web, March 1, 2002 from http://www.jstor.org.

Durant, Robert F., Jerome S. Legge Jr., and Antony Moussios, "People, profits, and service delivery: lessons from the privatization of British Telecom", *American Journal of Political Science*, Vol. 42, Issue 1 (Jan, 1998), 117-140. Retrieved from the World Wide Web, March 1, 2002 from http://www.jstor.org.

Moore, Michael K., and John R. Libbing, 1998. "Situational dissatisfaction in Congress: explaining voluntary departures", *The Journal of Politics*, Vol. 60, Issue 4 (Nov., 1998), 1083-1107. Retrieved from the World Wide Web, March 1, 2002 from http://www.jstor.org.

Neuhouser, Frederick. "Freedom, dependency, and the general will", *The Philosophical Review*, Volume 102, Issue 3 (Jul. 1993), pg. 363-395.

Ogunleye, Tolagbe, 1998. "Dr. Martin Robison Delany, 19th-Century Africana Womanists: reflections on his avant-garde politics concerning gender, colorism, and nation building", *Journal of Black Studies*, Vol. 28, Issue 5 (May, 1998), 628-649. Retrieved from the World Wide Web, March 1, 2002 from http://www.jstor.org.

Oskin, Becky, 2002. "St. Luke, Tenet sued by patients", *Pasadena Star-News*, Feb. 7, 2002.

Scott, John T. "The theodicy of the second discourse: the 'pure state of nature' and Rousseau's political thought", *The American Political Science Review*, Volume 86, Issue 3 (Sep. 1992), pgs. 696-711.

Stark, Andrew, 1997. "Beyond quid pro quo: what's wrong with private gain from public office?" *The American Political Science Review*, Vol. 91, Issue 1 (Mar., 1997), 108-120. Retrieved from the World Wide Web, March 1, 2002 from http://www.jstor.org.

Wilson, William J., 1996. "When work disappears", *Political Science Quarterly*, Vol. 111, Issue 4 (Winter 1996-1997), 567-595. Retrieved from the World Wide Web, March 1, 2002 from http://www.jstor.org.

The essays contained in this book were originally penned between 2000 and 2003, with additional development in 2013. The sources cited are from many scholars who did impeccable research with access to large factual databases and key "in the know" persons. What readers should notice is the path described in this book is now well traveled, and the world continues down the path at an accelerated speed, with no observable obstacles ahead. The fundamental principles mentioned in the essays and by scholars point to the fact that race really does matter and forms the foundation for the past, present and future distribution and control of wealth and power.

Anthropologists insist that race is not a biological phenomenon because individual differences among people within the same racial group far exceed those between racial groups... no group are quadrupeds, have eyes on the side of their heads or have elongated tails, etc. and can easily interbreed. On the other hand, anthropologists and archaeologists are able to distinguish the skeletons of the dead from different continents and conclude whether "them bones" represent Nordic versus African or Asian individuals... only they don't want to use the race card because it has become too emotionally charged and politically incorrect.

Let's summarize the historical and current relationships that impact the issue of race as a parameter in the expression of global political, economic and security concerns and the likely scenarios racism will take in the future, up to and including racial genocide.

1. Political racism has always disenfranchised racial minorities, and even after suffrage, laws were enacted to make it more difficult for minorities to vote, such as requirements to pass literacy tests and to show state issued identification cards. Even in the U.S. Constitution, blacks were counted as only as 3/5ths of a person. Many discriminatory laws were passed against blacks that included where they could sit on a public bus, which rest room or water fountain they could drink from, what "all white" restaurants, schools or establishments they were prohibited from entering and where they were allowed to live and who they could date and marry. Consequently, with the additional discriminatory laws, it is no surprise more blacks were jailed for defying unjust laws that enforced institutional racism.

2. Today, blacks account for 13.1% of the U.S. population, make up 40.1% of the almost 2.1 million male inmates in prison, while 43 African-Americans serve in the U.S. House of Representatives out of 435 members. As of 2012, there had been 1,931 members of the United States Senate, but only 6 were African American (wikipedia.com), however in 2013, 2 African Americans were appointed (not elected) to the U.S. Senate (Tim Scott from S.C. and "Mo" Cowan from N.C.). Roland Burris was an appointee who completed Barrack Obama's Senate term (www.senate.gov). Let's do the math... 10% in the House, and 2% in the Senate. Political racism? Other racial minority groups fair no better.

3. Economic racism is overt, pernicious and persistent. Detroit recently declared bankruptcy with over $18 billion in debt because "Motor City" just isn't rolling with jobs anymore as automakers and white flight followed the jobs out of the city. The unemployment rate in Detroit exceeds 20% (which means it's double due to the government's tricky underreporting by removing any "long term unemployed and discouraged workers" from the unemployment statistics. No wonder Detroit has become the second most violent city in America, with 40.1 percent of its population living in poverty.

4. The economic causes of racism are obvious... no jobs, little money (only what government programs contribute), and the results are predictable... neighbors prey on neighbors for survival and crime becomes rampant. Almost all of the cities with high crime rates also have a predominantly black population who are impoverished. This is the effect of economic racism where comparable predominantly white cities have good jobs and relatively low crime rates because when people are satisfied with the material things they possess, they need not rob their neighbors.

5. National security concerns have primarily focused on discovering potential Islamic terrorists due to obvious religious and racial profiling that is needed to narrow the focus on those most likely to share anti-American sentiments. However, in American cities with significant African American populations, police departments focus enforcement on high crime areas... usually those communities harboring high numbers of unemployed males, black teens, and black and Hispanic gangs who are responsible for the greatest portion of the violent crimes such as robbery, assault, and murder in addition to property crimes such as theft, selling/buying stolen property and drug related crimes. The underlying fear is whether Islamic extremists could make significant inroads to recruit racial minority members into their camps to pose a far-reaching national security threat to America. So far, al-Qaeda has focused on the recruitment of whites, such as the American Taliban senior al-Qaeda spokesman, Adam Gadahn (born Pearlman of Jewish descent). Edward Snowden, NSA contractor and whistleblower is white. Tim McVey, the Okalahoma bomber was white. The Boston Marathon bombing brothers are white (of Russian/Chechen descent). However, it

would not be unlikely that American Black Muslims are being watched to ascertain any possible contact or linkage to Islamist groups.

Racial minorities remain relatively powerless politically, economically and primarily pose a security threat to their own communities. Annually, blacks murder around 15,000 blacks and 1,600 whites and Hispanics. Unlike whites, they have never bombed anything to cause the deaths of innocent people. The victims of black crime are generally economically motivated, where the poverty of blacks drive them to rob and harm others... it is not religiously or philosophically derived.

The global conspiracy to eliminate most racial minorities and the poor from the face of the Earth as the ultimate solution to global problems of resource depletion, environmental pollution, overpopulation, poverty and crime is not just or necessary. Racism is never justified in any form, particularly as institutional policy. Rational effective and objective solutions to the world's problems already exist, but to implement them would require a more equitable redistribution of wealth, and the powerful elites will never stand for that... they would rather see racial genocide.

The most viable options to racial genocide is to offer the global elites a system where they can garner much greater benefits from the paradigm of plenty versus that of the zero sum game. It's time to play another game... that of raising the tide for all boats. How do we do that? The solutions are simple and exist right under our noses, and except for the racist desires of the most powerful elites, they can be done. How do we solve our global and national problems?

- Overpopulation policies as simple as the one-child policy should be instituted wherever population growth rates exceed global standards of replacement rate only. With a less than replacement population policy, explosive population growth in 3rd world nations can be put in check without exercising the racial genocide plan that is already in place using disease, genetically modified organisms, warfare, and eventually nuclear war.
- Crime is a direct consequence of poverty, unemployment, under education and the American culture of violence where firearms are easily attainable. Crime per se is not a racial propensity when the environmental causes of violence are removed.

- Environmental pollution and resource depletion is a direct outcome of human population growth that drives development, deforestation, species extinction, air pollution, global warming and water pollution. Restrain the growth of population and the other problems automatically decrease. Add far greater emphasis on alternative energies such as harnessing wind, water, solar and lightening and use technology to improve the efficiency of vehicles, homes and major appliances such a AC systems and refrigerators to reduce dependency on burning fossil fuels in electrical generation plants, vehicles, industries and commercial buildings.

- Every person can become a kinetic source of power generation to supply sufficient electricity to power their cell phones, LCD light sources for home use and small appliances such as portable radios and tablet computers. In addition, exercise gyms can harness all the people power to generate a significant amount of electricity to meet the lighting needs of the gym. All saving and conservation of fossil fuels resulting from more efficient and less polluting power sources, and harnessing human movement can contribute to a decreased dependence on the power grid for personal uses.

- The oil industry has been the primary perpetrator in blocking technological advances in alternative energies. If they wanted to, they could invest in those alternative energies, but why would they when pumping oil is what they do and how they've become the wealthiest companies and CEOs the world has ever seen? What can governments, energy competitors, and new technologies do to challenge and change the oil industry monopoly on global energy that affects almost every aspect of our lives from the fuels we use to the products we buy? First, remove all special tax breaks for these oil barons. Second, require them to invest a certain percentage of their profits to develop alternative energies. Third, improve the efficiency of vehicles both by reducing the size of engines and the speed limit – not popular, but the effects of global warming will be much more inconvenient. Fourth, reduce industrial pollution by requiring appropriate clean up.

- Genetically modify humans to create people who can fly and won't need cars or oil anymore... that will truly be freedom that no one can take away.

www.ingramcontent.com/pod-product-compliance
Lightning Source LLC
Chambersburg PA
CBHW082243310526
45795CB00013B/2016